WEEKENDS FOR TWO IN **SOUTHERN CALIFORNIA**

BILL GLEESON | PHOTOGRAPHS BY MARC LONGWOOD

weekends for two

IN

SOUTHERN CALIFORNIA

50 ROMANTIC GETAWAYS

CHRONICLE BOOKS

SAN FRANCISCO

ACKNOWLEDGMENTS

*The author wishes to thank Yvonne Gleeson,
for her research assistance and gender perspective;
Kari Gleeson, for her editing and manuscript
preparation; and Jeff Gleeson, "So Cal," so cool.*

*The photographer wishes to thank Sean and Caitlin
for doing without their dad for several weeks.*

Cover photograph:
Villa Toscana Bed and Breakfast

Library of Congress Cataloging-in-Publication
Data available.

ISBN 0-8118-4039-5

Manufactured in China.

Designed and typeset by Deborah Bowman

Distributed in Canada by Raincoast Books
9050 Shaughnessy Street
Vancouver, British Columbia V6P 6E5

10 9 8 7 6 5 4 3 2 1

Chronicle Books LLC
85 Second Street
San Francisco, California 94105

www.chroniclebooks.com

Table of Contents

Introduction

After being commissioned in 1993 to complement my book *Weekends for Two in Northern California* with a volume spotlighting Southern California, I had to struggle a bit to identify fifty romantic properties worthy of inclusion.

This time around, however, I discovered that a romantic renaissance had swept Southern California in the intervening decade. Instead of bending a rule or two to meet the magical quota of fifty, I was forced to whittle down an impressive list of close to one hundred south-state destinations deserving our attention.

The resulting revision represents a thorough overhaul showcasing the romantic best of today's Southern California. Although readers of previous editions of this book will recognize some familiar destinations, we've made way for more than twenty new discoveries, some of them recommended by travelers generous enough to share their favorites. We're also pleased to feature all-new photography in this revision, courtesy of traveling California lensman Marc Longwood.

ROOMS FOR ROMANCE

Our goal in creating this and the many other books in the *Weekends for Two* series is to take the mystery and guesswork out of choosing a destination for a special romantic getaway. During the course of our travels, we toured hundreds of inns and literally thousands of guest rooms in an effort to bring some definition to that often-maligned term *romantic*.

Our journeys have taken us from Catalina Island to the coast of Massachusetts, and from the gulf islands of British Columbia to the sleepy towns of New Mexico. We've slept in countless guest rooms and received letters from hundreds of readers. Following are some of the features we all like.

- Private bathrooms; a must in our opinion; we'll tell you if any are shared or detached.
- In-room fireplaces.
- Tubs and showers big enough for two; innkeepers in-the-know understand that a bathroom can be a romantic destination unto itself.
- Breakfast in bed; many traveling romantics don't fancy sharing a communal table with strangers.
- Feather beds and cushy comforters; need we say more?
- Comfortable couches, chaises, or love seats; the bed shouldn't be the only piece of furniture where two can be together.
- Lamps, sconces, and candles; overhead lighting isn't particularly romantic.
- Private decks, patios, or balconies; most of us enjoy the inspiration of the outdoors.
- Rooms where smoking is never permitted.

Although few, if any, of our chosen destinations offer this complete list of romantic ingredients, each offers at least some of these features. And we endeavor to point them out, along with the occasional critical caveat concerning noise, size and location, furnishings, and so on.

THE PRICE OF ROMANCE

If a special occasion is worthy of a special bottle of wine or meal, it also deserves a memorable place to stay and play. Accordingly, you should be prepared to invest a little more for a romantic room fit for a special occasion.

To help you plan your getaway budget, approximate rate ranges are included for most of the rooms we describe. These rates are always subject to change. If you're booking a weekend trip, please note that many establishments require two-night minimum stays. Some holidays command three-night minimums.

Rates (per high-season, weekend night for two friendly people) are classified at the end of each listing using the following circa 2004 ranges, not including tax:

Moderate: Under $200
Expensive: $200 – $300
Deluxe: Over $300

FINAL NOTES

No payment was sought or accepted from any establishment in exchange for being included in this book. We make the decisions about which properties to include and how they're described.

Please understand that we cannot guarantee that these properties will maintain furnishings or standards as they existed at the time of our visit. We very much appreciate hearing from readers if their experience varies with our descriptions. We always carefully consult reader comments as we plan revisions. Please send comments, suggestions, and ideas to Bill Gleeson in care of Chronicle Books at the address listed on the copyright page, or visit www.billgleeson.com.

Food, wine, and flowers may have been added to some rooms for photograph styling purposes. Some inns provide such amenities; others do not. Please ask when making a reservation whether these items are complimentary or whether they're provided for an extra charge.

DAYTIME DIVERSIONS

Encompassing the coast and rolling hills of beautiful SAN
LUIS OBISPO COUNTY, the South Central Coast is home
to Hearst San Simeon State Historical Monument, other-
wise known as Hearst Castle. For first-time visitors, we
recommend the "Tour Experience," which takes in an
opulent guest house, the magnificent indoor and outdoor
pools, and the ground floor of the castle, including the
refectory, billiard room, and theater. Romantic evening
tours are offered during certain periods. For more information,
visit www.hearstcastle.org.

THE PASO ROBLES WINE COUNTRY, home to more
than two dozen large and small wineries, can keep the two
of you entertained for an entire weekend.

Ocean lovers and walkers will enjoy the mile-long
boardwalk that hugs the bluff between Moonstone Beach
Drive and the Pacific in CAMBRIA.

The classic downtown of SAN LUIS OBISPO is also
worth a visit. Thursday night is the popular Farmers Market.

TABLES FOR TWO

Recommended PASO ROBLES dining choices include
Bistro Laurent and Alloro. Our CAMBRIA favorites include
Sow's Ear on Main Street and Robin's just around the
corner. Closer to the ocean is Moonstone Beach Bar and
Grill. Highly rated Mediterranean cuisine is served at
Ristorante Mare Blu in BAYWOOD PARK. Breakfast at
Apple Farm Inn in SAN LUIS OBISPO is always a pleasant
experience. The outdoor deck is the place to be on a warm
sunny morning. We also recommend the Buona Tavola and
Cafe Roma in San Luis Obispo.

THE SOUTH CENTRAL COAST

THE FACTS

Eight rooms, each with private bath, fireplace, CD player, television with videocassette and DVD player, and oversized spa tub. Complimentary full gourmet breakfast and afternoon wine and refreshments served at tables for two in on-site bistro restaurant. In-room spa treatments. Swimming pool. Disabled access. Two-night minimum stay required during weekends. Deluxe.

GETTING THERE

From Highway 101 in Paso Robles, follow Highway 46 east. Turn left on Buena Vista Drive. Follow to inn at end of road.

VILLA TOSCANA
4230 Buena Vista
Paso Robles, CA 93446
Telephone: (805) 238-5600
Web site: www.myvillatoscana.com

VILLA TOSCANA BED AND BREAKFAST

Wine country travelers who have ever bemoaned the scarcity of suitable romantic overnight lodgings along the Southern California wine roads have a new reason to visit Paso Robles. Villa Toscana Bed and Breakfast, which opened in 2002, gets our vote for the most romantic destination on the Central Coast. In fact, Villa Toscana is quite possibly the most enchanting in all of Central and Southern California.

Rivaling the finest properties in Napa and Sonoma Counties, it's the perfect nest for couples who enjoy topping off a day of wining with a memorable overnight experience. We even cut short our wine tour itinerary just to spend a few more precious hours in our suite.

For owners and longtime winemakers David and Mary Weyrich, Villa Toscana was the culmination of a dream to one day "bring the very best of Italy to California." They've succeeded in spades, from the inn's site on a gentle hillside to the artful Tuscan-themed design, not to mention the luxurious finishing touches that combine to make every room a work of romantic art.

The eight spacious accommodations are housed in one of a number of architecturally impressive buildings that dot a lushly landscaped, quiet country enclave that also includes the Martin & Weyrich Winery. The two-story guest room villa overlooks an expanse of vineyards and a seemingly endless vista of oak-studded hills and valleys. Next door is an impressive bistro, where guests gather to savor a glass of wine, enjoy an afternoon treat, or simply relax before the large fireplace or on the vineyard-view deck.

ROOMS FOR ROMANCE

Because each of the rooms is configured and styled in a distinctively impressive manner, we suggest you plan to make one or two trips each year until you've sampled them all. Our sumptuous sanctuary was the one-thousand-square-foot Zinfandel la Primitiva Suite, a second-floor room that we never wanted to leave. The walls are painted a pale yellow and trimmed in glossy white molding. At the rear of the suite stands a king-sized, partially draped and canopied bed heaped with multiple layers of coordinated fabrics and pillows.

At the foot of the bed stand a desk and a decorative wrought-iron divider that separates the sleeping and living areas. In the latter section, a plush couch sits before a raised fireplace, which is also visible from the bed. Two comfortable chairs and French doors flank the fireplace.

The tiled and marbled bathroom, a romantic destination itself, is spacious and soothing. There are dual sinks, a vanity, an oversized spa tub, and a separate shower with a drenching rain head. A complimentary bottle of the room's namesake wine completes the package.

The Viognier and Nebbiolo Suites, located on the first floor, are similarly spacious and feature step-down living areas with fireplaces and private patios.

All rooms share the impressive view of vineyards, hills, and valleys. The sun sets behind the guest room villa, creating magical sunsets and shadows on the hills and vines. Nightly rates for Villa Toscana go from the mid $300 range to around $400.

THE FACTS

Eight rooms, each with private bath; six with gas fireplaces. Complimentary full breakfast served at tables for two or four or delivered to guest rooms. Afternoon wine and refreshments. English-style pub with pool table and large-screen television. Disabled access. Two-night minimum stay required during holiday periods. Moderate to expensive.

GETTING THERE

From Highway 101, take Santa Barbara Road exit. Turn east on Santa Barbara Road and drive approximately one-half mile. Just past second stop sign, turn right on Hampton Court. Follow to inn at top of hill.

OAK HILL MANOR
12345 Hampton Court
Atascadero, CA
Telephone: (805) 462-9317;
toll-free: (866) 625-6267
Web site: www.oakhillmanorbandb.com

One of the many pleasures that come our way in charting romantic travel itineraries for California travelers is sleuthing out the hidden gems that have somehow escaped the radar of the masses. We made such a discovery in Atascadero, which for many Highway 101 travelers simply marks the halfway point between San Francisco and Los Angeles. The sleepy little town doesn't typically merit a stopover unless it's for gas or a quick bite to eat.

Next time you're plotting a Central Coast getaway, we recommend you consider a night or two at Oak Hill Manor, a handsome Tudor-style inn with eight distinctive and romantic guest rooms. Open only since 2000, the home-style inn sits on an oak-studded hill with beautiful local views. It's a particularly great home base for Paso Robles–area wine country tours. Hearst Castle is less than an hour away.

ROOMS FOR ROMANCE

The European honeymoon of proprietors Maurice and Rise Macare inspired the themes for the guest rooms, each of which is named and styled after a favorite country. Three of the suites—the Delft Suite, the St. Andrews Suite, and the Manor Suite— are located in the main house. The remaining five are found in the separate Carriage House located across a courtyard.

The most romantic of the main house rooms is the Manor Suite (upper $100 range), a spacious retreat whose Chippendale headboard, tea service, and pink, green, and white accents reflect a proper English theme. There's a sitting area with a fireplace and a couch, as well as a private balcony and a soaking tub big enough for two.

If golf is your game, by all means reserve the masculine, Scottish-themed St. Andrews Suite (mid $100 range), complete with golf-inspired art, antique golf clubs, and even a ball-return putting device.

In the Carriage House, one of our favorites is the Athenian Suite (upper $100 range). A lushly draped king-sized bed and a corner tub for two are the romantic centerpieces of this black-and-gold-colored retreat. There's also a fireplace and a small table and chairs set adjacent to a corner window.

Big enough for two queen-sized beds, the Florentine Suite (low $200 range) is ideal for a special romantic getaway. While the two of you hopefully won't need the second bed, this disabled accessible suite boasts a comfy couch set before a fireplace and a bathroom equipped with a whirl-pool tub and a separate shower. There's also a private patio.

Equally suited to a special getaway for two is the Alpine Suite (low $200 range), a spacious Carriage House room with a vaulted ceiling and a half-canopied king-sized sleigh bed. The two-sided fireplace is visible from both a comfortable sitting area couch and a whirlpool tub for two. This room also offers a private balcony.

THE FACTS
Sixty-nine rooms, each with private bath, television, telephone, and gas fireplace. Restaurant and swimming pool/spa. Disabled access. No minimum night stay requirement. Expensive to deluxe.

GETTING THERE
From northbound Highway 101 in San Luis Obispo, exit at Monterey Street and drive east to inn. From southbound Highway 101, exit at Monterey Street, turn left on Buena Vista, and left on Monterey Street.

The motel-dotted Highway 101 corridor through San Luis Obispo County has never been famous for cozy inns, but there is an exception to every rule. Located just a stone's throw from Highway 101, Apple Farm Inn is not only a great stopover for those heading to another destination, but also a romantic base from which to explore the San Luis Obispo area.

Guest rooms at Apple Farm borrow from traditional Victorian themes, characterized by wallpaper, wainscoting, and cozy, turreted sitting areas equipped with love seats, wing chairs, and window seats. Each room features a gas fireplace with a hearth, and a four-poster or canopied bed of brass, pine, or enamel.

ROOMS FOR ROMANCE

Two of the rooms, Millhouse A and Millhouse B (mid $300 range), are located above Apple Farm Millhouse, a working mill built over San Luis Creek. They both feature king-sized beds, sitting areas, balconies, and soaking tubs. Millhouse A overlooks the pool; Millhouse B has a view of the creek and surrounding trees.

Room 300 has an octagonal shape and is crowned with a skylight set in a turreted ceiling. The king-sized four-poster bed sits under a vaulted ceiling, and the bathroom is equipped with an oversized tub.

King-bedded rooms, most with canopies and some with sleeper sofas, are available in the low to mid $200 range.

Travelers on a budget might consider a room in Apple Farm's more motel-like Trellis Court, which offers many of the upscale features of the inn but at a lower price.

APPLE FARM INN
2015 Monterey Street
San Luis Obispo, CA 93401
Telephone: (805) 544-2040;
toll-free: (800) 255-2040
Web site: www.applefarm.com

THE FACTS
Eleven suites and seven rooms, each with private bath, microwave, refrigerator, gas fireplace, and telephone. Complimentary full breakfast served at tables for two in adjacent restaurant. Complimentary evening wine and cheese. Adjacent restaurant will deliver dinner to guest rooms. Disabled access. No minimum night stay requirement. Moderate to expensive.

GETTING THERE
From northbound Highway 101, approximately two hundred miles from Los Angeles, take Highway 1 exit toward Morro Bay. Exit Highway 1 at South Bay Boulevard (Los Osos/Baywood Park exit) and drive south for two miles to San Ysabel. Turn right and drive one mile to Second Street. Turn left; drive two blocks to inn.

BAYWOOD INN BED & BREAKFAST
1370 Second Street
Baywood Park, CA 93402
Telephone: (805) 528-8888
Web site: www.baywoodinn.com

BAYWOOD INN BED & BREAKFAST

It's a good thing we knew the address; we might well have mistaken the Baywood Inn Bed & Breakfast for a bayside office complex and driven right on by. Behind this contemporary corporate facade, however, we discovered more than a dozen enticing thematic rooms and suites.

Whatever your taste, chances are good there's a room here with your name on the door. Theme rooms include the Americana (upper $100 range), a celebration of red, white, and blue; the Southwest-style Santa Fe (upper $100 range); and the Appalachian (upper $100 range), patterned after a mountain cabin, with rough-sawn cedar beams, bark-covered tree limb furniture, and a river-rock fireplace. All rooms have queen-sized beds.

ROOMS FOR ROMANCE

While all of these accommodations were intriguing, we identified a few that seemed especially suited to traveling romantics. A colonial theme characterizes the Williamsburg (upper $100 range), a handsome bay-view room with a four-poster canopied bed and a brick fireplace. This upper-level room also has a separate dining area.

The Quimper Suite (upper $100 range), one of the inn's most romantic, has a cozy sitting area with a television, a couch, and a rocker, as well as a raised tiled fireplace. There's an adjacent bay-view eating area and a separate bedroom that's tastefully wallpapered and trimmed in blue.

On the lower level, the Queen Victoria Suite (upper $100 range) has a love seat for snuggling in front of a brick fireplace. The separate bedroom holds a brass bed.

Two bay windows offer a wide seashore panorama from the upper-level California Beach Room (upper $100 range). Tropical plants, sea-foam green carpet, and a glass topped, shell-shaped coffee table complete the scene. There's also a bedside fireplace.

The Avonlea and the Tex-Mex are both two-bedroom/two-bath suites (mid $100 range) that would work well for couples traveling together.

During our travels, the inn added three new rooms including the Providence Suite that features a two-sided fireplace and a bay view.

THE FACTS

Twenty-nine rooms, each with a private bath, spa tub, and gas fireplace. Complimentary continental breakfast served at tables in dining area or garden or delivered to your room. Complimentary afternoon refreshments. Communal spa. Disabled access. Two-night minimum stay required during weekends and holiday periods. Moderate to expensive.

GETTING THERE

Cambria is six miles south of Hearst Castle. Exit Highway 1 at Moonstone Beach Drive and follow to inn.

We discovered how Moonstone Beach Drive got its name when we ventured onto the seashore, aptly named Moonstone Landing, just across the street from this new inn. There we found visitors gazing not out to sea but intently at their feet and a beach composed of tiny ocean-sculpted pebbles and stones shaped like, well, moonstones.

This comfortable inn, with its handsome facade of shingles and travertine stone, is one of the newest additions to the string of overnight destinations that dot the eastern side of Moonstone Beach Drive, a one-and-a-half-mile coastal loop that parallels Highway 1 just north of Cambria village. There's no development on the ocean side of the road, which makes for some wonderful views from places like Moonstone Landing.

ROOMS FOR ROMANCE

For a romantic getaway, we recommend the inn's ten front-facing rooms, all of which feature dramatic sights and sounds of waves crashing just across the street. We prefer the front-facing rooms on the second level, which have decks; those on the ground floor have slightly less private connecting patios.

If these accommodations aren't available, we recommend a side-facing second-level room. These offer ocean views but do not have outdoor living spaces.

Rooms are moderately sized and have upscale Mission-style furnishings as well as attractive gas fireplaces whose stone facades match the inn's exterior. There's an in-ground communal spa on the rear patio.

MOONSTONE LANDING
6240 Moonstone Beach Drive
Cambria, CA 93428
Telephone: (805) 927-0012
Web site: www.moonstonehotel.com

THE FACTS

Six rooms, each with private bath, spa tub, and gas fireplace. Complimentary full breakfast served at communal table in ocean-view breakfast room. Complimentary afternoon refreshments. No disabled access. Two-night minimum stay required during weekends and holiday periods. Expensive.

GETTING THERE

Cambria is six miles south of Hearst Castle. Exit Highway 1 at Moonstone Beach Drive and follow to inn.

BLUE WHALE INN
6736 Moonstone Beach Drive
Cambria, CA 93428
Telephone: (805) 927-4647
Web site: www.bluewhaleinn.com

BLUE WHALE INN

Choosing from among the many lodging options along Cambria's Moonstone Beach Drive can be a daunting task. With an eye toward taking the guesswork out of your selection, we spent hours combing the one-and-a-half-mile loop for the best of the bunch. And while it's not a view property per se, the Blue Whale Inn easily emerged at the top of our list as the most romantic.

Distinctive among its more anonymous neighbors, the Blue Whale sets itself apart in both size and decor. Offering only six rooms, it's comparatively tiny. And the guest rooms feature some of the most stunning decor we've seen on the Central Coast.

The tidy, low-slung guest room complex is accessed via a walkway bordered by a garden area with benches, decorative rock, colorful paintings, and a waterfall pond.

The stylish gathering room, which overlooks the ocean, provides another comfortable haven for guests. A full gourmet breakfast is served here at a communal table in the adjacent dining area.

ROOMS FOR ROMANCE

Rooms at Blue Whale (mid $200 range) were designed by Mabel Shults, who also applied her considerable decorating skills to Apple Farm Inn and the Inn on Summer Hill (see separate listings).

Ms. Shults encourages innkeeping clients to devote a generous budget to individual room decor, and the owners of Blue Whale obliged. Guest rooms here are strikingly detailed, characterized by raised canopy beds with layered ruffles and comforters, bunches of throw pillows, decorative lamps (she prefers not to use overhead lighting), plantation shutters, crown molding, floral wallpaper, and pastel colors.

Each room has a distinctive look and is equipped with a gas fireplace, a love seat or couch, a small refrigerator, and a television (hidden in an armoire). Four rooms have king-sized beds; two have queens. Rooms 3 and 4 have slightly better partial views of the ocean.

Since our last visit, the inn's bathrooms have been redone and now feature marble floors and granite spa tubs for one.

THE FACTS

Eight rooms, each with private bath; seven with woodburning fireplaces. Complimentary full breakfast served at tables for two. Complimentary evening refreshments. No disabled access. Two-night minimum stay typically required during weekends. Moderate to expensive.

GETTING THERE

Cambria is six miles south of Hearst Castle. Take Burton Drive exit from Highway 1. Drive east for approximately one-half mile to inn.

J. PATRICK HOUSE
2990 Burton Drive
Cambria, CA 93428
Telephone: (805) 927-3812;
toll-free: (800) 341-5258
Web site: www.jpatrickhouse.com

J. PATRICK HOUSE

Unlike the contemporary seaside lodgings that seem to predominate Cambria these days, the J. Patrick House is a more traditional bed-and-breakfast hideaway with hints of old Ireland. The inn, an authentic log home, is nestled among pine trees above the village just to the east of Highway 1. Redecorated not long ago by proprietors Ann and John O'Connor, the inn is a cozy base from which to explore charming Cambria.

The town's first bed-and-breakfast inn, J. Patrick House consists of two buildings: a vintage log home in front and the adjacent Carriage House in which all but one of the guest rooms are housed. Rooms, which do not have televisions or phones, carry rates starting in the mid $100 range. Most have woodburning fireplaces.

ROOMS FOR ROMANCE

In Dublin (mid $100 range), a rear corner retreat on the first floor, a woodburning stove sits before a king-sized cherry wood sleigh bed. There's also a cozy window seat and a bathroom with a separate shower.

Next door is Tipperary (mid $100 range), a sunny rear-facing corner room with knotty-pine wainscoting and a window seat. The lovely centerpiece of this room is a locally crafted, queen-sized, draped four-poster bed. The bathroom holds a tub-and-shower combination.

Limerick (mid $100 range), a richly handsome second-floor corner retreat, has knotty-pine walls and ceiling, a window seat, and a brick fireplace. The private bath has a shower/bath combination.

Most often requested by romantics-in-the-know is Clare (around $200), the inn's largest and most expensive room, and the only one in the main building. Equipped with a king-sized cherry wood sleigh bed and a fireplace, the room is set under the eaves and features a log wall, a brick fireplace, and a peaceful view of the pines and gardens. The tiled bathroom has a view of trees and the garden. After 7 P.M., guests staying in Clare have exclusive use of the inn's living room and fireplace.

In-room massages may be arranged on request.

THE FACTS

Fourteen rooms, each with private bath, fireplace, spa tub for two, video and audio entertainment center, refrigerator, towel warmer, and microwave. Complimentary continental breakfast, afternoon wine and refreshments, and evening dessert served at tables for two. Communal rooftop spa. Room service available from restaurant next door. Disabled access. Two-night minimum stay required during weekends. Expensive to deluxe.

GETTING THERE

Cayucos is located on Highway 1 between Cambria and San Luis Obispo. From Highway 1, take Cayucos Drive exit and follow west to stoplight at Ocean Avenue. Cross Ocean Avenue; inn is on left at foot of Cayucos Pier.

CAYUCOS PIERPOINTE INN
181 Ocean Avenue
Cayucos, CA 93430
Telephone: (805) 995-3200
Web site: www.pierpointeinn.com

In earlier south-state sojourns, we never found a reason to linger very long in tiny Cayucos (pronounced Ki-YOU-kus). However, that's all changed since the recent opening of the luxurious Cayucos Pierpointe Inn. The fact that there's still not a lot going on in this little beach burg is reason enough to visit the new inn, which offers sufficient opportunities for a weekend's worth of cozy entertainment.

After searching the nation for the perfect location for an inn, proprietors Cary and Nicole Reibsamen found their spot right here in "downtown" Cayucos. The couple, traveling romantics themselves, created a comfortably stylish property at the foot of Cayucos Pier. Painted a tropical light green, the inn became an instant landmark on the town's sleepy main street. Many guests have turned out to be those who just happened to be passing through, spotted the inn, and found themselves drawn in to spend a night or two.

ROOMS FOR ROMANCE

We happened by within weeks of the inn's opening and were among the first to enjoy one of the second-floor ocean-view rooms. Room 204, our spacious and sunny, high-ceilinged retreat, features two lushly covered queen-sized beds and a small balcony overlooking the pier, the beach, and the ocean. Morro Rock is visible on a clear day.

Rooms have sleigh, four-poster, or canopied queen-sized or king-sized beds. All boast fireplaces and luxurious bathrooms with dual sinks and oversized spa tubs. Furnishings are high quality and include cushy chairs and ottomans and armoires that hide audio and video entertainment centers. Amenities include microwaves, refrigerators, evening turndown service, complimentary afternoon refreshments with wine, and complimentary evening dessert.

If you enjoy savoring the sea, our top recommendations are second-floor rooms 202, 203, and 204, which offer grand views. The most popular is room 202, an African-themed retreat with cathedral ceilings whose centerpiece is an exotic rattan bed with mosquito netting.

Although some of the inn's rooms face the main street and offer limited water views or street views, they're all luxuriously decorated. Regardless of your room location, the two of you have access to the rooftop spa and deck. Room 105 is completely accessible to disabled guests.

DAYTIME DIVERSIONS

In SANTA BARBARA, the stores, eateries, and theaters of State Street are bustling day and night. At the ocean end of State Street is Stearns Wharf and the beach. A bike path skirts a good portion of seashore. The Santa Barbara Zoological Gardens, located off Cabrillo Boulevard and Milpas Street, is home to exotic animals.

The Santa Barbara Mission, considered the queen of the California missions, is on upper Laguna Street near Mission Street. The mission is open daily, and visitors take self-guided tours of the museum, chapel, garden, and gift shop. Just over a mile north of the mission on Mission Canyon Road is the sixty-acre Botanic Garden with three miles of easy-to-walk trails.

SANTA YNEZ VALLEY is dotted with more than two dozen boutique wineries. Favorites include Sanford Winery in BUELLTON, Zaca Mesa Winery in LOS OLIVOS, and Carey Cellars in SOLVANG.

There are a number of art galleries worth exploring in tiny LOS OLIVOS, while the Danish heritage village of SOLVANG is another of this region's favorite destinations.

TABLES FOR TWO

In SANTA BARBARA, our innkeepers recommend Piatti, Stella Mare, Olio E Limone, Wine Cask, and La Marina at Four Seasons Biltmore. The dining room at El Encanto (see separate listing) offers wonderful city and ocean views. Mattei's Tavern in LOS OLIVOS and the Vintage Room in Fess Parker's Wine Country Inn and Spa are good choices in SANTA YNEZ VALLEY.

SANTA BARBARA AND
THE SANTA YNEZ VALLEY

THE FACTS
Twenty rooms, each with private bath; many with fireplaces and spa tubs. Complimentary full breakfast. Afternoon, and evening refreshments. Communal whirlpool spa. Day spa services. Moderate to deluxe.

GETTING THERE
From northbound Highway 101, take Arrellaga Street exit and follow for four blocks. Turn left on Chapala Street. Follow for one block to inn on corner of Chapala and Valerio Streets. From southbound Highway 101, take Mission Street exit. Follow for five blocks. Turn right on State Street and follow for three blocks. Turn right on Valerio Street and follow for one block to inn on right.

CHESHIRE CAT INN
36 West Valerio Street
Santa Barbara, CA 93101
Telephone: (805) 569-1610
Web site: www.cheshirecatinn.com

CHESHIRE CAT INN

It's always a good sign when we discover something new and different on a return visit to a favorite destination. This is typically an indication that the owners are focused on keeping things fresh and updated. While the spirited Alice in Wonderland theme remains at Cheshire Cat Inn, much has changed since our first visit not long after the inn's 1985 opening.

Among the changes is the property's size. The Cheshire Cat has grown fatter and happier as it ages and now includes a third venerable Santa Barbara residence. In addition to the elegant main house and the neighboring "second house," the enclave offers four delightful new rooms in the James House, an impressive century-old Victorian that has recently been restored.

Also new is a menu of spa services that include massages, facials, and body treatments. Alice never had it this good.

What haven't changed are the inn's grounds, which still overflow with the colorful and lush flora that flourish in this remarkable climate. There's also an outdoor spa tub set in a gazebo.

ROOMS FOR ROMANCE

While our favorite rooms carry tariffs in the mid $200 range and up, romantics on a budget will appreciate the handful of mainhouse hideaways offered in the mid to upper $100 range. Among these is the intimate Dormouse, which features a gas fireplace and a bathroom with a shower. In the same price range is March Hare, which has a pretty windowed sitting area with two chairs.

The nicest rooms in the main house are the Cheshire Cat Suite and Caterpillar. The Cheshire Cat Suite (mid $200 range) is a handsome retreat with a vaulted ceiling decorated in burgundy, gold, and cream hues. The suite holds a king-sized bed and a spa tub for one.

The split-level Caterpillar (low $200 range) has two window seats, one of which is in the lower-level sitting area. Guests here enjoy a private deck with garden and mountain views.

In the second house, we can recommend Queen of Hearts (mid $200 range), furnished in wicker and Laura Ashley trimmings. There's also a spa tub, a private entrance, and a brick patio. A blue-tiled spa tub is the centerpiece of Eberle (mid $200 range), which also features a queen-sized bed and a gas fireplace.

In the James House, our top pick is Unicorn (low to mid $200 range), which has a spa tub for two, a corner bay window, and a charming balcony with two chairs.

The inn also features two great coach house rooms called Tweedledum and Tweedledee, and a pair of cozy cottages.

THE FACTS

Twenty-three rooms, each with private bath, gas fireplace, soaking tub, and balcony or patio. Complimentary continental breakfast buffet taken at tables for two. Complimentary evening refreshments. Lap pool and fitness room. In-room spa services. Free parking. Disabled access. Two-night minimum stay required during weekends and holiday periods. Expensive to deluxe.

GETTING THERE

From northbound Highway 101, take Carrillo Street exit and turn left on Carrillo Street. Turn right on Garden Street and follow to inn on right. From southbound Highway 101, take Garden Street exit. Turn right on Garden Street and follow to inn on left.

INN OF THE SPANISH GARDEN

915 Garden Street
Santa Barbara, CA 93101
Telephone: (805) 564-4700;
toll-free: (866) 564-4700
Web site: www.spanishgardeninn.com

INN OF THE SPANISH GARDEN

Inn of the Spanish Garden is our top recommendation for those who enjoy spending their days prowling Santa Barbara's charming and vibrant downtown district. When the shops, restaurants, and theaters along State Street roll up the sidewalk at the end of the day, guests need walk only three blocks to their love nest in one of the city's most charming and romantic inns. Tucked away on a relatively quiet side street with underground parking, Inn of the Spanish Garden is situated such that downtown-bound guests can park their cars and stash the keys in a drawer.

From the street, the newly constructed Spanish Mediterranean–style inn might easily be mistaken for a private residence. Signage is discreet, and guests enter the establishment via a short set of steps and a porch. Once beyond the handsome interior public areas, you'll cross an inner courtyard that opens to a trio of white plaster-walled guest buildings, newly built but exuding the requisite Santa Barbara charm.

ROOMS FOR ROMANCE

One of the wonderful new South Coast properties that have opened since our last edition, Inn of the Spanish Garden was designed with today's traveler in mind. Guest rooms are unusually spacious and equipped with all the romantic comforts we covet.

Our second-floor hideaway for a night was room 11 (upper $200 range), which oozes Santa Barbara style, with plaster walls, touches of tile, arches, and nary a square angle to be seen. The king-sized bed faces a fireplace and an armoire housing a television. A covered balcony overlooks the swimming pool. The skylit bathroom is tiled and equipped with a tub big enough for two and a separate shower. This room is classified as an "executive" accommodation. "Deluxe" rooms are less expensive (starting in the low-to-mid $200 range).

Room 23 is a spacious two-room "junior suite" (mid $300 range). The bedroom holds a king-sized bed and an oversized dresser. The separate living room is furnished with two chairs that face a fireplace and a desk.

At the time of our visit, the inn offered romance packages that included a cozy room, breakfast in bed, and in-room massages. For a romantic dinner, we can recommend, from personal experience, an outdoor table at the enchanting La Playa Azul Cafe, which can be accessed at the rear of the inn's property.

31

THE FACTS

One hundred twenty-two rooms and suites, each with private bath and CD player. Complimentary full breakfast served in guest dining room. In-room meal service available. Two swimming pools and communal spa. Fitness center and day spa. Disabled access. Two-night minimum stay required during weekends and holiday periods. Moderate to deluxe.

GETTING THERE

From Highway 101, exit at Castillo Street toward harbor. Turn right on Castillo Street and left on West Cabrillo Boulevard.

Set between the picturesque harbor and popular Stearns Wharf along the city's bustling beachside boulevard, Hotel Oceana is one of the many new and noteworthy Santa Barbara destinations that opened their doors not long after the millennium.

Not to be confused with its more intimate sister property in Santa Monica (see separate listing), Santa Barbara's Hotel Oceana is a perfect hideaway for couples who enjoy the ocean (the beach is just across the street) and the endless shopping potential of State Street, only one block away. Eight miles of paths, which beckon walkers, skaters, and bikers, also await your explorations.

Drawing its inspiration from Santa Barbara's pervasive Mission-style architecture, the hotel offers more than one hundred rooms and a number of on-site communal comforts including two swimming pools, a fitness and spa facility, and a patio with an outdoor fireplace.

ROOMS FOR ROMANCE

Guest rooms owe their style to Kathryn Ireland, who decorated the homes of such notables as Caroline Kennedy Schlossberg and actors Steve Martin and Fran Drescher. At Hotel Oceana, the guest accommodations are decorated in what might best be described as beach casual. Rooms feature fabrics in summery hues of blue, yellow, red, or green. Beds are covered with Italian linens, and bathrooms, typically separated from the bedroom by a graceful archway, are small but functional and equipped with upscale fixtures.

For a special romantic getaway, we recommend a room in the "superior ocean view" category. These carry tariffs ranging from the high $200 range to the mid $300 range. For an even more romantic experience, consider a suite. These run from the low to mid $300 range to around $400. The hotel also offers partial ocean-view rooms as well as those that face garden or courtyard areas.

Although all rooms feature high-speed Internet access, we recommend, in the spirit of a romantic getaway, that you leave the laptop at home.

HOTEL OCEANA
202 West Cabrillo Boulevard
Santa Barbara, CA 93101
Telephone: (805) 965-4577;
toll-free: (800) 965-9776
Web site: www.hoteloceana.com

SIMPSON HOUSE INN
121 East Arrellaga Street
Santa Barbara, CA 93101
Telephone: (805) 963-7067
Web site: www.simpsonhouseinn.com

THE FACTS

Fourteen rooms and suites, each with private bath, seven with fireplaces; four with tubs for two. Complimentary full breakfast served on veranda or delivered to your room. Complimentary evening wine and refreshments. Free bicycle rentals. In-room spa services available. Local fitness club privileges at additional per-guest charge. Disabled access. Two-night minimum stay required during weekends; three-night minimum stay during holiday periods. Expensive to deluxe.

GETTING THERE

From Northbound Highway 101, take Garden Street exit and turn right. Turn left on Gutierrez Street and right on Santa Barbara Street. Follow for thirteen blocks. Turn left on Arellaga Street and follow to inn on right. From southbound Highway 101, take Mission Street exit and turn left. Follow Mission Street for six blocks and turn right on Anacapa Street. Turn left on Arellaga Street and follow to inn on left.

SIMPSON HOUSE INN

They call Mission Santa Barbara the queen of California's missions. In our opinion, Simpson House Inn is the queen of Southern California's bed-and-breakfast inns. In one of the region's most romantic cities, there is no more romantic place to stay than this lovely Victorian landmark. Occupying an enchanted acre hidden from the street by walls and mature greenery, the Eastlake Victorian-style property offers a collection of fourteen intimate accommodations, including garden cottages and luxury suites in a reconstructed antique barn.

ROOMS FOR ROMANCE

The main house contains seven individually decorated rooms, each offering a different guest experience. Arguably the nicest of these is the Robert and Julia Simpson Room (mid $400 range), boasting elaborate wallpaper, a queen-sized antique bed, a sitting area, and a private bathroom with an old-fashioned clawfoot-tub-and-shower combination.

On the ground floor is the Garden Room (upper $300 range), set under oak trees and offering a private patio and a view of the lawns and garden. Accessed by French doors, the queen-bedded room has an antique pine floor and Oriental rugs, a vaulted ceiling with a skylight, and a bay window seat.

One of the inn's least expensive accommodations (mid $200 range), the Katharine McCormick Room is a small, nicely decorated retreat with a queen-sized bed and two cushy chairs. The lowest-priced room, called Mary Simpson, has a detached private bathroom.

A painstakingly reconstructed old barn contains four romantic suites offered in the $500 range. Each has a king-sized bed, a love seat, a woodburning fireplace, and videocassette players.

Greenwich Cottage is one of the freestanding cottages, each opening onto a private fountain courtyard. This unit has a handsome river-rock fireplace that can be seen from the carved bed. In addition to queen-sized feather beds and fireplaces, the three luxurious cottages (mid $500 range) all have in-room spa tubs for two.

Located within walking distance of Santa Barbara restaurants, shops, and attractions, the Simpson House offers free use of bicycles for city and neighborhood touring.

EL ENCANTO HOTEL AND GARDEN VILLAS
900 Lasuen Road
Santa Barbara, CA 93103
Telephone: (805) 687-5000
Web site: www.elencantohotel.com

THE FACTS
Eighty-four rooms, each with private bath, television, and telephone, thirty-nine with fireplaces. Swimming pool and tennis court. Restaurant. Disabled access. Two-night minimum stay required during weekends; three-night minimum stay required during holiday periods. Expensive to deluxe.

GETTING THERE
From Highway 101, exit at Mission Street and follow signs to Mission Santa Barbara. Veer right at fork onto Alameda Padre Serra for one-half mile. Veer left at next fork onto Lasuen. El Encanto Hotel is on right.

Intimate details of a romantic getaway may smolder in the memory for years, but the images of a particular destination can fade with time. Unless the place is as special as El Encanto.

A personal favorite destination for many years, El Encanto (Spanish for "the enchantment") is quintessential Southern California, with tiled roofs, sweeping views of the distant ocean, swaying palms, quaint cottages, and tropical grounds. Its privacy—most cottages are secluded along narrow pathways between mature trees and shrubbery—has lured many famous couples since Hollywood's Golden Age.

Accommodations at El Encanto are varied. Sharing the ten-acre hillside are cozy, board-and-batten cottages dating from the 1930s, whitewashed adobe villas, and condominium-style buildings constructed during the 1970s. Most rooms feature French country decor.

ROOMS FOR ROMANCE

Room 322 has a private porch, a separate bedroom with a king-sized bed, and a wonderful living room with a couch and a fireplace. This room is offered in the mid $500 range.

Room 301 (mid $200 range) is a secluded freestanding villa situated near the pool. Done in a tasteful green color scheme, it's equipped with a king-sized bed, a fireplace, and a sitting area.

If you're wondering why El Encanto has been designated a historical landmark, try cottage 237, a cozy older bungalow (mid $200 range) with a queen-sized bed, a fireplace, and a kitchenette. From personal experience, we can also highly recommend cottage 316 (with French doors and in a private hillside setting), villa 306 (with an adobe fireplace and a glorious view), and villa 329, actually a freestanding cottage suite with a spacious porch surrounded by lush gardens.

While they lack some of the historic charm and intrinsic character of the villa suites, the more contemporary-style courtside villa rooms (mid $200 range) are nicely furnished, and many offer ocean and city views from porches and patios.

During the daytime, guests often chart a course for Santa Barbara's charming downtown, tour the nearby mission, or lounge at the hotel pool. Evenings at El Encanto are quiet hours, the waters of the trellis-fringed pond rippled only by resident goldfish. Couples stroll hand in hand along the winding brick pathways or cuddle in hushed conversation in the swinging love seats that dot the grounds. Not long after nightfall, the walkways empty as guests retreat to their cottages.

THE FACTS

Sixty-one rooms and suites, each with private bath, video-cassette player, and refrigerator. Complimentary continental breakfast served in lobby area. Swimming pool and spa. Fitness room. Restaurant and bar. Room service. Limited disabled access. Two-night minimum stay required during weekends; three-night minimum stay during holiday periods. Expensive to deluxe.

GETTING THERE

From Highway 101, take Olive Mill Road exit (east). Inn is at corner of Coast Village and Olive Mill Roads.

MONTECITO INN
1295 Coast Village Road
Santa Barbara, CA 93108
Telephone: (805) 969-7854
Web site: www.montecitoinn.com

MONTECITO INN

Despite its location some eighty-five miles north of Tinseltown, the Montecito Inn is an elegant reminder of Hollywood's Golden Age.

The year was 1928; Charlie Chaplin was an established star and garnering extravagant wages for his work in silent films. Chaplin, along with fellow movie star Roscoe "Fatty" Arbuckle, reportedly invested $300,000—a fortune at the time—to build this stylish hotel in the hills just outside Santa Barbara.

As legend has it, a young Richard Rodgers paid a visit sometime later. Inspired by a couple tossing a coin into the hotel's garden wishing well, the famous tunesmith penned the classic song "There's a Small Hotel (With a Wishing Well)."

The wishing well didn't survive, but the years have been kind to the Montecito Inn, which has undergone thoughtful renovations that have preserved the hotel's charm while introducing contemporary niceties that keep today's discerning travelers coming back. In our opinion, the inn ranks among Santa Barbara's most romantic getaway destinations.

ROOMS FOR ROMANCE

With its arched windows, coved ceilings, and other ornate architectural trimmings, the inn carries a European feel. In the guest rooms the furniture is French provincial, and chairs, tables, and beds are covered in tasteful fabrics. Well-equipped bathrooms feature hand-painted tiles. All rooms have televisions, videocassette players, refrigerators, and telephones with voice mail and data ports. Deluxe queen rooms with corner mountain views are offered in the low $200 range. Rooms with king-sized beds are offered in the low $200 range. A junior studio suite with a king-sized bed, two bathrooms, and a sitting area is available at a nightly rate of around $300.

A more recent renovation brought seven luxury suites offering from one to three bedrooms. For that special romantic getaway, we recommend a one-bedroom luxury suite. You'll be treated to separate living and bedroom areas, a custom-designed fireplace, and a large bathroom lavished with Italian marble and a spa tub. Plan on spending in the mid $400 range for a deluxe king suite.

The Montecito Café, located on the premises, serves lunch and dinner, as well as an appetizer menu. Meals also may be ordered through room service.

THE FACTS

Thirty-eight cottages, rooms, and suites, each with private bath, fireplace or woodburning stove, king-sized bed, CD player, complimentary snacks, and porch or deck; several have private spas. Swimming pool. Tennis courts. Fitness center. Walking trails. Restaurant and bistro. In-room spa services available. Disabled access. Smoking is allowed and pets are welcome for an additional fee. Two-night minimum stay required during weekends; three-to-four-night minimum stay during holiday periods. Deluxe.

GETTING THERE

From Highway 101 south of Santa Barbara, exit San Ysidro Road; drive northeast (away from ocean) to San Ysidro Lane. Turn right and follow to ranch.

SAN YSIDRO RANCH

For generations, San Ysidro Ranch has been tugging at the heartstrings of the romantically inclined rich and famous. A look at the guest register says it all. The John F. Kennedys honeymooned at the ranch, actors Laurence Olivier and Vivien Leigh recited their marriage vows on the beautiful grounds, and rocker Mick Jagger sought seclusion here.

Because each cottage, room, and suite has a personality all its own, there's no pat description for the ranch. Having served as a guest retreat for the last century, the complex is an attractive and luxurious mix of old and new. And where else can you expect to find your name engraved on a little sign outside your door?

ROOMS FOR ROMANCE

Accommodations at San Ysidro Ranch range from around $400 to thousands of dollars per night, depending on size and view. Canyon Rooms (around $400) have king-sized beds and private patios, and they share a common outdoor deck.

Slightly better suited to a special romantic get-away are the Ranch Rooms (around $500), which are larger, more stylish studios offering more opulent bathrooms. Superior Rooms and Cottages (around $600) are nicer still; some of these have separate living rooms.

The ranch's Deluxe Cottages have cozy sitting areas with comfy furnishings and private outdoor spas. Although they carry lofty tariffs of around $700, these are among the most popular rooms at the ranch.

The grand, two-bedroom Kennedy honeymoon cottage fetches around $1,900 per night.

SAN YSIDRO RANCH
900 San Ysidro Lane
Montecito, CA 93108
Telephone: (805) 969-5046;
toll-free: (800) 368-3788
Web site: www.sanysidroranch.com

THE FACTS

Sixteen rooms, each with private bath, gas fireplace, goose-down comforter, single-person spa tub, and balcony or patio. Complimentary full breakfast served in dining room or delivered to your room for an additional fee. Complimentary afternoon wine and refreshments and evening dessert. Communal spa. Two-night minimum stay required during weekends and holiday periods. Disabled access. Expensive to deluxe.

GETTING THERE

From Highway 101, take Summerland exit. Follow frontage road (along east side of highway) north a short distance to inn.

INN ON SUMMER HILL
2520 Lillie Avenue
Summerland, CA 93067
Telephone toll-free: (800) 845-5566
Web site: www.innonsummerhill.com

Guests at the Inn on Summer Hill face a pleasant, albeit difficult choice, particularly on a sunny Southern California afternoon. Although the distant beach beckons from your balcony, the guest rooms here are so comfortable you may find yourself opting for a cushy sofa.

ROOMS FOR ROMANCE

Cited by our readers as one of Southern California's most romantic destinations, the Inn on Summer Hill offers tantalizing rooms with canopied beds, goose-down comforters, corner fireplaces, and sunny balconies. Accommodations here will remind you of those luscious retreats pictured in decorating magazines—a dream bedroom come true.

For example, in room 5 downstairs, a delightful combination of stripe and floral drapes cascades down the four posts of a king-sized bed. Red-and-white gingham bows are tied to each post. The patterns are carried over to the double dust ruffle, pillow shams, tablecloth, and lamp shades.

The stripe and floral combination is featured in other rooms including room 12, done in hues of blue, mauve, and white. Room 4 (green with touches of red) has hardwood floors, a fainting couch, and a king-sized bed with an ornate German antique headboard carved with the inscription *Gute Nacht*. Each room holds an antique chest.

Rooms here carry rates in the mid $200 range. Those with king-sized beds and balconies are slightly more expensive than those with queen-sized beds and patios. The wonderful Deluxe Suite with a vaulted pine ceiling, two ocean-view balconies, and a separate living room and dining area is available in the mid $300 range.

Guests who prefer breakfast in the privacy of their room receive a tray filled with a hot breakfast entree, homemade breads, cereal, fresh fruit, juice, and muffins. (There is a small fee for this service.) A similar spread is served at a communal table in the dining room or cozy tables for two.

Reminiscent of a New England country estate, the Inn on Summer Hill sits on a hillside in the oceanside village of Summerland, just ten minutes south of Santa Barbara. Rooms have ocean and island views. Although Highway 101 can be seen from the upstairs guest rooms (landscaping blocks the road view from the main level), traffic noise does not present a problem, thanks to soundproofing.

THE FACTS

*Twenty-one rooms, each with private bath, gas fireplace;
five with spa tubs for two. Complimentary continental
breakfast. Morning paper delivered to room. Complimentary
bottle of wine and wine tasting at Fess Parker Winery and
Vineyard. Restaurant. Swimming pool and spa. Day spa
nearby. Disabled access. Two-night minimum stay required
during weekends. Deluxe.*

GETTING THERE

*From southbound Highway 101 south of Los Alamos, take
Highway 154 exit and drive two miles to hotel on Grand
Avenue. From northbound Highway 101 just past Santa
Barbara, take Highway 154 exit and drive twenty-eight miles
to hotel on Grand Avenue. Los Olivos is approximately one
hundred forty miles north of Los Angeles, approximately
five miles north of Santa Barbara, and five miles from
Solvang.*

Veteran actor Fess Parker, who immortalized Davy Crockett in the 1950s and founded a winery in Santa Ynez Valley in the late 1980s, has more recently turned his attention to the hospitality trade. Since our last visit to this tiny burg, the lovely Los Olivos Grand Hotel has been acquired by the Parker clan and rechristened as Fess Parker's Wine Country Inn and Spa.

While its charming turret and gables suggest a feeling of yesteryear, you won't confuse the hotel with the many pre-1900 buildings that dot the town's main street. This is very much a contemporary hotel offering romantic luxuries unknown during Los Olivos' earlier days.

If the inn appears smaller than its twenty-one rooms, it's because about half the accommodations, along with the swimming pool and spa, are across the street in a separate building. The hotel's public areas, registration desk, and highly rated restaurant are on the first floor of the main wing. There are ten guest rooms upstairs.

FESS PARKER'S WINE COUNTRY INN AND SPA

2860 Grand Avenue (P.O. Box 849)
Los Olivos, CA 93441
Telephone: (805) 686-5749
Web site: www.fessparker.com

ROOMS FOR ROMANCE

French country is the pervasive theme at the Wine Country Inn, whose redecoration in the recent past was overseen by Fess Parker's wife, Marcella. Top-of-the-line accommodations are the spacious two-room Grand Suites (mid $400 range). Fireplaces warm the separate bedrooms, which also hold a small table and chairs. Separate spacious living rooms are furnished with a couch and chairs.

Other rooms (mid $300 range) feature either two queen-sized beds or one king-sized bed. These rooms are nicely appointed with two cushy chairs, fireplaces, armoires, and small tables with two chairs.

The inn also operates a respected on-site restaurant and a day spa located just steps away.

45

Fourteen rooms, each with private bath and audio/video entertainment system; twelve with gas fireplaces; thirteen with spa tubs. DVD library. Complimentary full breakfast served at communal tables and tables for two or four. Complimentary evening wine and refreshments. Communal spa and sun deck. Fitness suite with spa services. Disabled access. Two-night minimum stay required during weekends and holiday periods. Expensive to deluxe.

GETTING THERE

From Highway 101 at Buellton, drive east on Highway 246 and follow past Solvang. Look for green Santa Ynez town signs and turn left on Edison Street. Drive three blocks and turn right on Sagunto Street. Inn is on left. From Santa Barbara, drive north on Highway 154. Turn left on Highway 246, right on Edison Street, and right on Sagunto Street.

Thank goodness for the growth of Santa Ynez Valley's wine industry. As the number of wineries and wine road travelers has increased, so have the overnight options. We remember when it was difficult to find a suitable room anywhere in the region. Today's travelers have multiple impressive overnight options. Our pick for the valley's most romantic wine country hideaway is Santa Ynez Inn, a new Victorian-style charmer with rooms that rival any we've seen in Southern California in terms of romantic ambience.

Open only since 2001, the rambling structure strikes a handsome nineteenth-century pose with its turret, gables, covered porches, and gingerbread trim. Step inside and you'll be impressed with how the Victorian theme has been nicely balanced with contemporary comforts. Although you'll find high ceilings, old-fashioned chandeliers hanging from detailed rosettes, and antiques reminiscent of days gone by, you'll no doubt appreciate the spaciousness and brightness, not to mention amenities such as CD players, Internet data ports, and whirlpool tubs. It's Victorian to a proper and tasteful point.

ROOMS FOR ROMANCE

For a memorable romantic getaway, we're partial to the rooms categorized as "superior king" (around $300) and "deluxe" (around $300 for a queen and mid $300 range for a king), as well as the "junior suites" (around $400).

We're partial to the sound of water, so one of our favorites is room 104, a ground-floor accommodation whose French doors open onto a small, front-facing patio adjacent to a fountain. This richly draped room has a king-sized iron bed and a fireplace.

At the high end, junior suite 210 boasts an ultra-romantic king-sized bed with carved wooden posts and canopy and pretty fabrics. Furnished also with an ornate armoire and dresser, this room has a fireplace. Junior suite 202, which occupies the multiwindowed cupola, is another good romantic choice.

Room 208, with its antique bed and dark armoire, boasts a private deck with a valley view. Four rooms have steam showers.

SANTA YNEZ INN
3627 Sagunto Street (P.O. Box 628)
Santa Ynez, CA 93460
Telephone: (805) 688-5588;
toll-free: (800) 643-5774
Web site: www.santaynezinn.com

THE FACTS

Fifteen rooms, each with private bath (three of the rooms are in adjacent annex); seven rooms have woodburning fireplaces. Complimentary full breakfast served in dining room. Complimentary afternoon wine and refreshments. Restaurant serves dinner. Disabled access. Two-night minimum stay required during weekends; three-night minimum stay during many holiday weekends. A service charge is added to bill at checkout. Expensive.

GETTING THERE

From northbound Highway 101, exit at Highway 154 and follow for about thirty miles. Take Edison-Baseline exit. Turn right at stop directly on Baseline Avenue and follow for just over two miles to inn on left. From southbound Highway 101, take Highway 246/Solvang exit to Alamo Pintado Road. Turn left and follow for three miles to Baseline Avenue. Turn right and follow to inn on right.

THE BALLARD INN

2436 Baseline Avenue
Ballard, CA 93463
Telephone: (805) 688-7770;
toll-free: (800) 638-2466
Web site: www.ballardinn.com

Blending Victorian styling with the modern niceties of a small contemporary hotel, the Ballard Inn is one of Southern California's best-kept secrets. It's a picture-postcard country inn. A covered porch runs the length of the inn, under clapboard gables and turrets, with a little balcony tucked here and an arched window there. Every embellishment is here, right down to the daisies and white picket fence.

Step inside and you won't be disappointed. The four attractive common rooms on the main floor set the stage for the upstairs guest chambers, each designed to commemorate the people, places, and events that have shaped the Santa Ynez Valley.

ROOMS FOR ROMANCE

The Mountain Room, the largest and most popular in the house (upper $200 range), offers stunning views of the mountains through windows on three sides and from a private balcony. The room is furnished with bent-willow tables and a king-sized bed, and is warmed by a fireplace.

One of the most unusual guest retreats you'll find anywhere in Southern California is Davy Brown's Room (low $200 range), designed in honor of a former Ballard townsman who rode with the Texas Rangers and trapped with Kit Carson. Three of the room's walls are beamed and mortared to resemble a log cabin. This room, which has rug-covered hardwood floors, also has a stone fireplace and early American antiques.

Other historic themes are celebrated in the Western Room, where an old pair of cowboy chaps adorn the wall. The Jarado Room (low $200 range) features a Native American motif.

Morning sun floods the bay-windowed sitting area of the Vineyard Room (mid $200 range), which features a king-sized bed and a blond hardwood floor. Cynthia's Room (mid $200 range), a tribute to the so-called first lady of Ballard, features a fireplace and a bed covered with a double-wedding-ring duvet with a down comforter.

Another attraction of the Ballard Inn is the food. Guests are treated to a full breakfast, cooked to order and served in an antique-filled dining room. The granola and baked goods are made on the premises. Cafe Chardonnay restaurant is also on site.

Before checking out, be sure to sign your wine cork and throw it in the basket downstairs for luck. Maybe the two of you will be lucky enough to return.

THE FACTS

Forty rooms, each with private bath, television, and telephone; two rooms with fireplaces. Complimentary European-style buffet breakfast (ham, cheese, pastries, and beverage) served each morning in the courtyard lounge. Complimentary coffee and tea room service. Cafe Provence for guest dining. Disabled access. Moderate to deluxe.

GETTING THERE

From Highway 101, take Solvang exit at Buellton. Follow signs to Solvang. Inn is on Mission Drive in heart of town. Solvang is approximately one hundred thirty-five miles north of Los Angeles.

THE INN AT PETERSEN VILLAGE

While many Solvang visitors are satisfied with a brief morning or afternoon shopping encounter, we continually meet people who admit to an enduring romantic fascination with this European-style village. For these folks, a visit to Solvang won't be complete without an overnight stay in the half-timbered Inn at Petersen Village.

Located in the center of town, the longtime family-owned-and-operated inn is the cornerstone of Petersen Village, which includes a Danish bakery and coffee shop, two restaurants, and more than twenty specialty shops.

After negotiating the village's crowded streets, step inside the quiet, softly lit inn for a refreshing change. Danish antiques and black-vested bellboys create a charming atmosphere.

ROOMS FOR ROMANCE

Many of the guest rooms feature exposed beams and chintz fabrics. Most are furnished with raised and canopied king- and queen-sized beds (with stepping stools) and rich, traditional furnishings. Televisions are hidden inside armoires.

Rooms have either courtyard, village, or garden views. Lest the sight of American autos on Mission Drive remind you that you're still in Southern California, we recommend, to prolong your Old World experience, the second-floor rooms facing the quaint interior courtyard. Courtyard King rooms, which feature comfortable sitting areas, carry tariffs in the mid $200 range.

Of particular note is the three-level suite that occupies the ornate, half-timbered tower. The Tower Suite (around $300) holds two bathrooms, a dual spa tub, a living room with a fireplace, a king-sized four-poster bed, and a spa tub for two.

THE INN AT PETERSEN VILLAGE
1576 Mission Drive
Solvang, CA 93463
Telephone: (805) 688-3121;
toll-free: (800) 321-8985
Web site: www.peterseninn.com

FERRY INFORMATION

Most people travel to AVALON (Catalina Island's main community) by boat, and there are multiple carriers from the mainland. Catalina Express offers several daily sailings between Long Beach/San Pedro and Avalon. The cruise takes a little over one hour. The Catalina Flyer makes the journey from Newport Beach to Avalon in about seventy-five minutes. Plan on spending around $40, more or less, for a round-trip ticket, depending on which cruise line you choose. Tickets may be purchased online.

For terminal directions, cruise details, and other information, call the Catalina Island Chamber of Commerce and Visitors Bureau at (310) 510-1520 or visit the Web site at www.visitcatalina.org. You can also fill out a request for the bureau's informative Catalina visitors guide. Another useful Web site is www.catalina.com.

DAYTIME DIVERSIONS

In addition to village shops, the harbor beach is a popular destination, especially on sunny days. Savvy beachgoers walk down early and lay claim to the best spots on the sand with their beach towels, then head back to bed for a few extra winks.

If you'd like to see more of CATALINA, rent a golf-type cart (there's a rental shop near the boat terminal) and explore the inland region of the island on your own. To probe the island's interior reaches, you'll need to buy a ticket for an open-air tram tour. Other tours here include a glass-bottom boat ride, a coastal cruise to Seal Rocks, a flying-fish boat tour (at night), and a tour of the famous Avalon Casino. You can also rent bicycles in AVALON or arrange a horseback ride.

TABLES FOR TWO

Our CATALINA recommendations include the Channel House, Cafe Prego, the Catalina Country Club, and the Blue Parrot. The Landing Bar and Grill in El Encanto Market Place has a great bay-view patio and serves casual island fare. Your innkeeper can help arrange a dinner cruise.

CATALINA ISLAND

THE FACTS

Six rooms and suites, each with private bath (room 5 has a partial bath); four rooms with fireplaces. Complimentary full breakfast, deli lunch, and refreshments included. Complimentary shuttle between boat terminal and heliport. Complimentary personal golf cart provided for use in and around Avalon. No disabled access. Two-night minimum stay required during weekends and holiday periods. Deluxe.

GETTING THERE

When you reach island boat terminal, call the inn for shuttle service.

INN ON MT. ADA
P.O. Box 2560
Avalon, CA 90704
Telephone: (310) 510-2030

INN ON MT. ADA

Having spent the better part of a year searching out Southern California's most romantic getaways, we had been overwhelmed with inspiring views and sensual surroundings by the time we reached Long Beach Harbor. Cruising to Catalina on the last leg of our sojourn, we wondered whether we'd already seen the best of the bunch. Then we spied the Inn on Mt. Ada sparkling like a jewel on the hillside. As we headed up the hill on an island taxi, we had a distinct feeling that the best had been saved for last.

We were right. Savoring what is one of California's most inspiring views, from our bed no less, we decided life couldn't get much better.

This opulent Georgian-style mansion was built by the late chewing-gum mogul and Chicago Cubs owner William Wrigley Jr., who bought the whole island, reportedly sight unseen. He built the house for his wife, Ada. After the Wrigley years, the home sat abandoned for some time until a few years ago when innkeepers Susie Griffin and Marlene McAdam stepped in and restored it to its former glory.

All room rates include breakfast, deli-style lunch, refreshments, and personal use of a golf cart. Midweek and off-season rates are less expensive.

ROOMS FOR ROMANCE

Mr. Wrigley's private bedroom and living room now compose the Grand Suite, which carries a weekend and summer rate in the mid $600 range. Included are an opulently furnished sitting area, a queen-sized canopied bed in the sleeping chamber, a private bath, a marble fireplace, and a private harbor-view terrace furnished with lounge chairs.

Ada Wrigley had her own adjacent private bedroom suite and bath on the second floor. Now known as the Queen's Aviary (mid $500 range), it features a tile-trimmed fireplace, a sitting area, and a romantically draped queen-sized four-poster bed.

The inn's best view (in our opinion) is offered from the Windsor Room. The four-poster bed in this intimate chamber is raised high enough to provide the two of you with vistas of Avalon village and harbor as well as the California coastline across the channel. The lovely view is also offered from the private bath, which has a radiator heater and a shower/bath with original fixtures, including Mr. Wrigley's extra faucet for regulating an old salt-water system (it no longer works). This corner room, which has a gas fireplace, is available in the mid $500 range.

THE FACTS

Fifteen rooms and suites, each with private bath; all but one have fireplaces. Complimentary continental breakfast served in courtyard. Beach chairs and towels. No disabled access. Two-night minimum stay required during weekends; three-night minimum stay during holiday weekends. Moderate to deluxe.

GETTING THERE

Hotel is located on Avalon's main street in heart of village. Hail a taxi at boat terminal or walk to hotel, luggage permitting. Hotel is about a five-minute walk from boat terminal.

HOTEL VISTA DEL MAR

417 Crescent Avenue (P.O. Box 1979)
Avalon, CA 90704
Telephone: (310) 510-1452
Web site: www.hotel-vistadelmar.com

HOTEL VISTA DEL MAR

If California has a mecca for romantics, Catalina Island is it. Whether it's for a honeymoon, anniversary, or weekend splurge, most couples owe it to themselves to make this passion pilgrimage at least once.

While the name Hotel Vista del Mar is among the newer additions to the lodging scene of Avalon, the building has been around for some time. The Vista del Mar is a comparatively upscale hostelry that blossomed from what was known for many years as the Camp Bravo Hotel.

Sporting an open-air atrium and a breezy Mediterranean style, the hotel contains only fifteen rooms, each with a tiled wet bar, a gas fireplace raised for romantic viewing from bed, and a private tiled bath. The beach is just steps away.

ROOMS FOR ROMANCE

If a water view is important, the hotel has two prime bay-vista suites (mid $300 range). These accommodations, which measure more than four hundred square feet, feature balconies, sitting areas with couches, raised fireplaces, and spa tubs for two placed to take advantage of the view.

If the suites are booked, consider one of the six ample Courtyard Deluxe Rooms (low $200 range), which face the atrium and have queen-sized beds, spa tubs, and sitting areas. Smaller Courtyard Rooms with fireplaces, sitting areas, and tub-and-shower combinations are available for around $200.

SNUG HARBOR INN
108 Sumner Avenue (P.O. Box 2470)
Avalon, CA 90704
Telephone: (310) 510-8400
Web site: www.snugharbor-inn.com

THE FACTS
Six rooms, each with private bath, king-sized bed, fireplace, CD player, air conditioning, fresh flowers, and deep spa tub. Complimentary continental breakfast and evening wine and cheese served in lobby area. No disabled access. Two-night minimum stay required during weekends; three-night minimum stay during holiday weekends. Expensive.

GETTING THERE
Inn is located on corner of Crescent and Sumner Avenues. Crescent Avenue is the community's main street and parallels Avalon Bay. Those who pack light and ride the ferry can walk from dock to inn. Taxi service is also available.

Created by the same folks who operate Hotel Vista del Mar (see previous listing), Snug Harbor Inn is one of Avalon's newest and nicest boutique inns. Discreetly occupying the second level of a commercial building in the heart of the village overlooking the harbor, the tiny, six-room hostelry is aptly named. What it lacks in size, however, it makes up for in romantic charm. All rooms have king-sized beds, fireplaces, televisions, CD players and spa tubs, as well as special touches like Egyptian cotton sheets, fresh flowers, and terry slippers. Tasteful nautical knickknacks create a laid-back beach vibe. The inn also provides beach chairs and towels.

Snug Harbor Inn is also conveniently located, just a short stroll from the ferry dock, across the street from the beach, and steps from shops and restaurants.

ROOMS FOR ROMANCE

The best ocean views are offered from the Santa Catalina Room (low to mid $300 range) and from the San Nicolas Room (high $200 range). The most desirable and largest is the Santa Catalina Room, decorated in cheery yellow and white tones and boasting two sets of bay windows. One window has a romantic cushioned seat for two.

Our other favorite, the San Nicolas Room, is painted deep blue with contrasting white wainscoting and trim. The palm tree and harbor view from this room is particularly stunning.

The other four rooms have partial ocean views. Among these, the Anacapa (low $200 range), is a good-sized hideaway featuring a nautical theme in white. In the Santa Barbara Room (low $200 range), there's a beach scene painted on the wall behind the bed. At about two hundred twenty square feet, the Santa Cruz Room (around $200) is the smallest room. This bright and cozy retreat features double windows.

Bathrooms are upscale, well equipped, and lit by either a window or skylight. The countertops are granite, and each bathroom has a deep spa tub.

Rates at Snug Harbor Inn are considerably lower during Catalina Island's quieter months of November through April.

DAYTIME DIVERSIONS

If the two of you would like a taste of showbiz while in the greater LOS ANGELES area, consider joining the audience of a television show taping. Audiences Unlimited handles ticket distribution for numerous shows. You can request tickets by visiting www.audiencesunlimited.com. Paramount Television also produces shows taped before studio audiences. For ticket information, call Paramount's Guest Relations Department at (323) 956-1777. Tickets for *The Tonight Show* are available through the mail. Send a self-addressed, stamped envelope to *The Tonight Show*, 3000 West Alameda Avenue, Burbank, CA 91523. Send well in advance of your scheduled getaway and provide a brief list of desired dates.

TABLES FOR TWO

Giorgio Baldi and Beach House, both on West Channel Road, are great SANTA MONICA choices. In MALIBU, try Duke's Malibu or Allegria, both on Pacific Coast Highway. We also recommend Granita, Wolfgang Puck's fabulous Malibu restaurant.

BEVERLY HILLS–bound couples might ask their concierge to assist with reservations at the ever popular Spago. At Temple, also in Beverly Hills, the menu features Korean cuisine with Brazilian flavors.

The Ivy on North Robertson Boulevard near Beverly Boulevard in LOS ANGELES is popular among celebs. In NEWPORT BEACH, consider The Ritz, and in DANA POINT, our innkeepers recommend Luciana's.

In LAGUNA BEACH, a romantic choice is French 75, while OJAI visitors will enjoy the Ranch House Restaurant and the Maravilla Restaurant at Ojai Valley Inn and Spa.

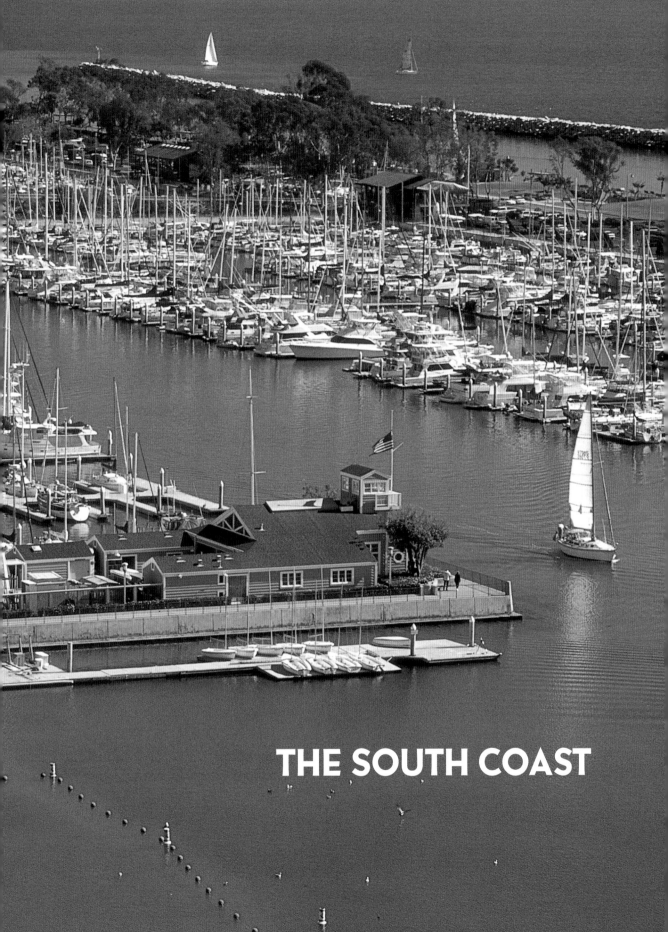

THE SOUTH COAST

THE FACTS

Twenty-nine rooms, each with private bath with double sink, gas fireplace, spa tub, terry robes, CD player, and mini-refrigerator stocked with complimentary refreshments. Complimentary breakfast (delivered to your room for an additional charge) and afternoon wine and refreshments. Exercise room. Free bicycle rentals. Disabled access. Two-night minimum stay required only during certain holiday periods. Moderate to deluxe.

GETTING THERE

Inn is located one block west of Highway 1 on Street of the Blue Lantern, twenty minutes south of the Orange County Airport.

Relaxing in the lobby of the fully booked Blue Lantern Inn one summer Saturday evening, we found it difficult to ignore the constant parade of unlucky couples who, lacking reservations, were politely turned away, two by two.

Sporting an enchanting Cape Cod facade with lots of interesting angles and a gabled slate roof, the Blue Lantern perches at the edge of a Dana Point cliff overlooking the yacht harbor and coastline. Although its bluff-top location prohibits direct beach access, the inn more than makes up for this small disadvantage with its decor, amenities, food, and charm.

ROOMS FOR ROMANCE

The most romantic accommodations are the dozen or so described as Pacific Edge rooms. These cliff-side rooms offer ocean and harbor vistas and either a patio or balcony. A second- or third-floor Pacific Edge hideaway with a balcony carries a tariff in the mid $200 range. Patio rooms run a bit less.

A selection of Harbor View King rooms is offered for around $200. Nonview rooms run in the upper $100 range.

The fabulous Tower Suite (around $500), with a thirty-foot-high vaulted ceiling, a 180-degree view, a telescope, a stereo, and a balcony is a favorite among Southern California newlyweds and is often booked months in advance for weekends.

The Blue Lantern's Pacific Edge and Harbor View rooms (not to mention the decadent suite) scored a solid A on our romantic report card. All the ingredients for a passionate escape are in place here: fireplaces (although not woodburning), spa tubs for two in spacious bathrooms that are destinations in themselves, Pacific sunsets, terry robes, and a private breakfast in your room. Ready, set, start packing!

BLUE LANTERN INN

34343 Street of the Blue Lantern
Dana Point, CA 92629
Telephone: (714) 661-1304;
toll-free: (800) 950-1236
Web site: www.foursisters.com

THE FACTS

One hundred fifty-seven rooms and suites, each with private bath, private ocean-view balcony, CD player, and twice-daily maid service; about half the rooms have tubs for two. Restaurant. Day spa. Swimming pool. Disabled access. Smoking is allowed; nonsmoking rooms are available. Two-night minimum stay required during weekends; two-to-three-night minimum stay during holiday periods. Deluxe.

GETTING THERE

Resort is located near heart of Laguna Beach on South Coast Highway 1, approximately twenty minutes south of Orange County Airport, approximately one hour south of Los Angeles International Airport, and approximately seventy minutes north of San Diego Airport.

SURF AND SAND RESORT
1555 South Coast Highway
Laguna Beach, CA 92651
Telephone toll-free: (888) 869-7569
Web site: www.surfandsandresort.com

SURF AND SAND RESORT

Three cheers for the thoughtful readers who recommended we take a look at this extraordinary oceanfront property. After an overnight visit we agreed that Surf and Sand Resort deserved a spot on our list of the south state's most romantic destinations.

We typically seek out smaller and more intimate accommodations, but Surf and Sand rated high on our romantic scorecard despite its comparatively large 157-room size. We can't imagine any couple being able to resist the ocean views and Catalina sunsets afforded from these crisp and clean rooms. This is Southern California at its seaside best.

ROOMS FOR ROMANCE

Chances are you'll initially miss the bleached wood furnishings, separate sitting areas, and armoire with television. Instead, you'll head straight for the balcony and beckoning blue Pacific.

Bathrooms are contemporary, supplied with bathrobes, a second telephone, and a quality sound system. Many offer glass-enclosed showers and marble tubs for two.

Our room was in the Towers building, a nine-story wing perched just feet from the surf. The only thing visible from our room was water. The smaller Surfside building is similarly situated. The Seaside Terrace building is set back behind and above the swimming pool, and these rooms, while boasting the nice straight-on ocean views, don't offer the sweeping vistas provided from the aforementioned buildings. Rates start in the mid $300 range. At the time of our travels, the resort offered two-night romantic getaway packages with champagne for two, breakfast, and dinner ranging from around $500 to the mid $700 range depending on the season.

Guest amenities include a restaurant, a full-service day spa called Aquaterra, and an ocean-view swimming pool with a glass-enclosed deck and poolside bar. The hotel also offers five hundred feet of beautifully sandy beach conveniently accessed by stairs. Laguna Beach's charming boutiques and galleries are within walking distance.

THE FACTS

Eleven rooms and suites, each with fireplace, private bath, and sunken tub. Complimentary continental breakfast. 21 Oceanfront Restaurant. Disabled access. No minimum night stay requirement. Expensive to deluxe.

GETTING THERE

From Interstate 5, take Highway 55 toward Newport Beach. Follow signs to Newport Pier. Inn is at base of pier, approximately twenty minutes from John Wayne Airport.

DORYMAN'S OCEANFRONT INN

Contained entirely on the second level of a beachfront building and reached only by a small, private eleva-tor, Doryman's Inn just might be the South Coast's best-kept romantic secret. Unlike some hotels that invest heavily in showy public areas and scrimp on guest rooms, Doryman's has no grand lobby. The lion's share of attention has been lavished on the impressive bedchambers.

ROOMS FOR ROMANCE

All rooms have French glass, antiques, rich draperies, beveled mirrors, sexy sunken tubs, tiled fireplaces and carved mantelpieces, brass fixtures, and skylit bathrooms of Italian marble. Many of the inn's beds are canopied and draped with yards and yards of soft fabric. The best of everything is con-tained in room 8, one of the inn's most romantic (mid $300 range). Features include a king-sized canopied bed, a gas fireplace, an ocean view, and a spa tub for two.

Room 6 also has a sunken spa tub as well as a beautiful king-sized bed with mirrored headboard, and access to the outdoor patio. In the Bellagio Room (high $300 range), a couch sits at the foot of a king-sized bed. This grand room also features a spa tub for two and a wet bar.

Rooms 1, 2, and 3 have fine ocean views along with the Doryman's standard luxury features. These carry rates in the low $200 range. Room 5 (around $200), with an ocean view, a queen-sized bed, a fireplace, and a sunken tub, is the inn's least expensive.

Be sure to request one of the rooms facing the beach if an ocean view is important to you. Some rooms have better views than others.

DORYMAN'S OCEANFRONT INN
2102 West Oceanfront
Newport Beach, CA 92663
Telephone: (949) 675-7300
Web site: www.dorymansinn.com

THE FACTS

One hundred seventy-five rooms, each with private bath. Restaurant. Swimming pool. Disabled access. Smoking is allowed in guest rooms. No minimum night stay requirement. Expensive to deluxe.

GETTING THERE

From Freeway 10, take Fourth Street west exit. Turn right on Fourth Street and drive one block to Colorado. Turn left on Colorado and follow to Ocean Avenue. Turn left on Ocean and follow to hotel on right.

LE MERIGOT
1740 Ocean Avenue
Santa Monica, CA 90401
Telephone: (310) 395-9700;
toll-free: (888) 539-7899
Web site: www.lemerigothotel.com

The selection of destinations in this volume attests to our fondness for quiet, small hotels and inns offering only a handful of rooms along with healthy doses of peace and privacy. However, sometimes we crave a fix of luxury, served up in large, full-service luxury hotels that spoil guests with niceties like room service, on-site dining and entertainment, a highrise view, spa services, and, as is the case with Le Merigot, even twice-daily housekeeping service.

A J.W. Marriott property, Le Merigot is all we look for and more. Centrally located in downtown Santa Monica, it's within easy walking distance of the city's famous landmarks including the ocean bluff Palisades Park, Santa Monica Pier, and the lively and trendy Third Street shopping promenade of shops, bars, and restaurants.

There's also much to keep you occupied at the property itself, where diversions include a fitness center, a swimming pool, and a European day spa equipped with a eucalyptus steam sauna, a dry sauna, and a whirlpool, and offering dozens of body treatments. A terrace bar and a well-respected French restaurant complete the Le Merigot package.

ROOMS FOR ROMANCE

Not surprisingly, rooms at Le Merigot are priced primarily according to view. A number of rooms feature city or mountain views, and these command prices in the upper $200 range. We prefer those rooms classified as "deluxe ocean view." These rooms, priced in the mid $300 range, feature large patios or balconies from which to savor the ocean and those marvelous Santa Monica sunsets.

All rooms feature Le Merigot's signature "cloud nine" beds, which are dressed in Frette linens and covered with down duvets and feather pillows. Furnishings include oversized chairs and couches. In the unlikely event that boredom sets in, electronic amenities include a trio of telephones, high-speed Internet access, CD players, and ample-sized televisions. The hotel also promises room-service breakfasts within fifteen minutes.

For a romantic getaway, make sure you ask for a king-sized bed as many rooms have either a king-sized bed or two full-sized beds. We also suggest that you ask about corporate rates or packages when you call to book a room.

Couples who enjoy traveling with their pets will appreciate the hotel's "pet-friendly" policy, which allows Fido to share your room, provided you pony up a refundable damage deposit and a nominal nonrefundable cleaning fee.

THE FACTS

Sixty-three suites, each with private bath, kitchen, and lanai or patio. Complimentary continental breakfast delivered to your room. Swimming pool. Fitness center. Lounge and room service. Valet parking. Disabled access. Two-night minimum stay typically required only during certain holiday periods. Deluxe.

GETTING THERE

From Interstate 10, take Fourth/Fifth Street exit and follow to left at fork in ramp. Turn right on Fourth Street and left onto Colorado Avenue. Turn right on Ocean Avenue and follow to hotel on right.

HOTEL OCEANA

849 Ocean Avenue
Santa Monica, CA 90403
Telephone: (310) 393-0486;
toll-free: (800) 777-0758
Web site: www.hoteloceana.com

Hotel Oceana was designed around a fundamental concept we wholeheartedly endorse: "Santa Monica is best enjoyed in the reclining position." Whether it's a chaise by the pool or an Adirondack chair on your private lanai, there are plenty of places for you to test the vision yourselves. This fresh and laid-back property is one of our favorite South Coast destinations.

Set on a bluff at what the hotel describes as "the quiet end of Ocean Avenue," Hotel Oceana shares the rarified air of one of Santa Monica's most exclusive neighborhoods. Originally a condominium complex, the hotel emerged not long ago from a million-dollar upgrade that brought refurbished guest accommodations and other improvements. The beach is a short walk away across Pacific Coast Highway. Other Santa Monica attractions are also within walking distance.

ROOMS FOR ROMANCE

Because it used to be a residential enclave, Hotel Oceana boasts some of the largest accommodations we found in our Southern California travels. Averaging more than eight hundred square feet, the sixty-three colorful and breezy guest rooms offer plenty of room to relax and recline. There are fully equipped gourmet kitchens, spacious bedrooms boasting wonderful Italian linens, marble bathrooms, and separate living rooms with high-tech media centers and art deco–inspired furniture. Most rooms have semiprivate lanais or balconies and face either the pool courtyard or the ocean.

For a one-bedroom suite with a swimming-pool view, plan on spending around $400. Just a few dollars more brings a partial ocean view. Rooms with a slightly better ocean view are offered in the low $400 range while rooms with extraordinary ocean views command about $500. For a romantic getaway, we suggest you request a room with a king-sized bed; some are furnished with two full-sized beds.

The property also features an open-air lounge, a swimming pool, and a fitness center. Room service is provided by a nearby upscale restaurant.

THE FACTS

Fourteen rooms and suites, each with private bath. Complimentary full breakfast served at tables for two or in your room. Complimentary afternoon tea and cookies and evening wine and cheese. Hillside spa. Free bicycle rental. In-room spa services available. Disabled access. Expensive to deluxe.

GETTING THERE

Follow Interstate 405 to Interstate 10 west to Pacific Coast Highway (Highway 1). Drive north on highway to third traffic light (West Channel Road). Make a hard right onto West Channel Road and drive one-quarter mile to inn on left.

Built in the early 1900s as a family residence, the Channel Road Inn is our recommended destination for Santa Monica–bound travelers who prefer to balance the hustle and bustle of the city with a home style overnight alternative.

Constructed in Colonial Revival style—somewhat a rarity on the West Coast—the handsome manor features shingles painted a sky blue and an ornately carved Craftsman-style door. Of the fourteen rooms and suites, five have views of the ocean.

ROOMS FOR ROMANCE

Room 11 (mid $200 range) is decorated in an English garden motif with bleached pine furnishings, including a matching four-poster queen-sized canopied bed. Guests have a view of the garden and ocean. Room 9 has an ocean-view sitting area and a fireplace.

Room 12 (mid to upper $200 range) occupies a quiet corner with a view of the ocean. A coffee-and-white color scheme is accented with warm, dark wood. The king-sized bed has a rattan headboard; from the bed, guests have their Pacific view.

The two of us sampled the inn's spacious bridal suite (room 6; mid $300 range), where a spa tub for two is set beneath a window and a queen-sized, four-poster, canopied bed is heaped with lots of Battenburg lace. The separate living room has a nonworking fireplace, a comfy sofa, and two lovely Queen Anne chairs.

Room 3 has a fireplace and a spa tub for two. Room 1, a small chamber with a tiny bathroom, faces the back of the property and opens onto a sunny deck.

CHANNEL ROAD INN
219 West Channel Road
Santa Monica, CA 90402
Telephone: (310) 459-1920
Web site: www.channelroadinn.com

THE FACTS
Twenty-one rooms, each with private bath. Complimentary continental breakfast included. Disabled access. Two-night minimum stay during weekends; three-night minimum stay during holiday periods. Moderate to deluxe.

GETTING THERE
Inn is on ocean side of Pacific Coast Highway, ten and a half miles north of Interstate 10 in Santa Monica.

CASA MALIBU INN ON THE BEACH
22752 Pacific Coast Highway
Malibu, CA 90265
Telephone: (310) 456-2219

CASA MALIBU INN ON THE BEACH

A South Coast original, Casa Malibu Inn has been hosting guests long enough to describe one of its rooms as "Lana Turner's favorite." In operation for more than a half century, this venerable property is laid back and informal, evoking images of yesteryear while providing contemporary comforts the late Lana could have only dreamed about. For example, a handful of guest rooms have cozy gas fireplaces, and all have been retrofitted with data ports. Room service is provided by Wolfgang Puck's nearby restaurant.

ROOMS FOR ROMANCE

Notwithstanding the inn's exclusive address and location, rooms at Casa Malibu Inn are a bargain, with rates at the time of our visit starting in the low $100 range for a garden-view room. For those planning a special romantic getaway, we recommend a room with a water view. Our favorites are the popular beachfront rooms (low $200 range) whose private decks sit just inches above a broad, gentle swath of prime Malibu beach. Rooms in the "ocean-view" category are located upstairs and also feature decks that look out over the rooftops to the ocean.

The Catalina Suite (low $200 range), which played host to screen legend Lana Turner, is an upstairs minisuite equipped with a fireplace, a separate sitting room, a kitchen, and views of the garden area and the ocean.

The most deluxe accommodation is the Malibu Suite (mid $300 range), a romantic beachfront retreat offering a kitchen, a fireplace, a spa tub, and a spacious deck.

Rooms with kitchens can be reserved for just a few additional dollars and with a three-day minimum. All rooms have small refrigerators and coffeemakers.

Rooms are equipped with either king-sized beds or two double beds. The inn also provides beach towels, beach chairs, and umbrellas, as well as guest membership at a local health spa and golf course.

THE FACTS

Forty-seven rooms, each with private bath, private balcony, ocean view, and videocassette player; most have fireplaces. Guests have access to sandy swimming beach. Complimentary continental breakfast buffet served on patio. Limited room service. Two-night minimum stay required during weekends and holiday periods. Disabled access. Expensive to deluxe.

GETTING THERE

Inn is located on beach side of Pacific Coast Highway (Highway 1), near Malibu Pier and Alice's Restaurant, at north end of town. Los Angeles International Airport is approximately thirty-five minutes away. John Wayne Airport is about an hour-and-a-half drive from inn.

MALIBU BEACH INN
22878 Pacific Coast Highway
Malibu, CA 90265
Telephone: (310) 456-6444;
toll-free: (800) 4MALIBU
Web site: www.malibubeachinn.com

MALIBU BEACH INN

The Malibu Beach Inn holds the distinction of being the first hotel to be built on this part of the southern coast in almost a half century. About as close to living in Malibu as most of us will ever get, the inn offers guests a taste of the comfortable life that residents of this exclusive enclave enjoy.

The inn is set so close to the seashore that about all that can be seen from most windows is the blue ocean. The beach is reached via stairs from a tiled patio just outside the lobby.

ROOMS FOR ROMANCE

Don't expect antiques, flowing fabric, and lace at Malibu Beach Inn. Furnishings here are simple, contemporary, and functional. The layout, similar from room to room, consists of a queen-sized bed; a sofa bed; a coffee table facing a tiled gas fireplace with a raised hearth; and a Philippine-made cane wall unit housing a wet bar, a refrigerator, and drawers. Art is mostly limited to pastel striping and an occasional shell painted on the wall.

Third-level rooms all have vaulted ceilings with recessed lighting and uncovered balconies big enough for a couple of chairs and a lounger. Second-level rooms all have covered ocean-view balconies with furniture. First-floor rooms have balcony spas.

For the most memorable romantic getaway, we recommend a full oceanfront room with a sitting area, a fireplace, and a soft-sided spa tub for two placed on the balcony. These Beachcomber Rooms start in the lower $300 range. Rooms with grand ocean views but without a balcony spa are available for around $300. Partial oceanfront and pier-view rooms with fireplaces are offered in the upper $200 range.

THE FACTS

Three hundred ninety-seven rooms and suites, each with private bath with deep soaking tub and oversized shower, CD and DVD player, room service, and twice-daily house-keeping services. Swimming pool, health spa, fitness center, restaurants, and lounge. Disabled access. Smoking is allowed; nonsmoking floors are available. No minimum night stay requirement. Deluxe.

GETTING THERE

From Interstate 405, exit east on Wilshire Boulevard and follow for approximately four miles to hotel. From Interstate 10, exit on Robertson and drive north for approximately three miles. Turn left on Wilshire Boulevard and follow for approximately one mile.

THE REGENT BEVERLY WILSHIRE

9500 Wilshire Boulevard
Beverly Hills, CA 90212
Telephone: (310) 275-5200
Web site: www.fourseasons.com;
click on "find a hotel"

THE REGENT BEVERLY WILSHIRE

It has been the choice of emperors and empresses, kings and queens, princes and princesses. It's also a favorite among our own Hollywood royalty. For example, the celebrity "king" of romance, Warren Beatty, was so taken that he moved in during his widely chronicled bachelor years.

The Regent Beverly Wilshire, a local landmark since the late 1920s, still reigns as one of Beverly Hills' shining stars. Located in the heart of Beverly Hills at Wilshire Boulevard and tony Rodeo Drive, the hotel, a Four Seasons property, commands a most coveted spot within one of the world's most exclusive shopping areas.

ROOMS FOR ROMANCE

Accommodations are spread among the stately historic main building and the more contemporary Beverly Wing, which was added in 1971. A domed porte cochere, lit at night by thirty-eight gaslight lanterns from Edinburgh Castle, joins the two buildings.

As you might expect, there are accommodations here that are literally fit for a king, a president, or a movie star. The posh Presidential Suite, for example, carries a nightly tariff of more than $5,000. The Veranda Suite (around $1,200), which Warren Beatty called home for a time, is privately situated on the tenth floor. The fabulous, five-thousand-square-foot Penthouse Suite was the setting for *Pretty Woman* starring Julia Roberts and Richard Gere. If you have to ask about the rate, you can't afford it.

For those of us who don't have unlimited resources, the hotel offers spacious rooms in the Beverly Wing—some nearly four hundred square feet in size—with king-sized beds and luxurious marble baths, at rates starting around $400. Rooms with balconies overlooking the pool are offered in the low $400 range. At the time of our travels, the hotel offered romantic escape packages.

Our suite for a special night, room 820, was illuminated by six tall windows, some of which offered a view of Century City. A sitting area with a love seat and an armchair was at one end, and a desk and another comfortable chair were positioned at the other. A luscious king-sized bed sat in the middle before an armoire with a television. The large marble bathroom, entered through French doors, held a spacious glass and marble shower, a separate deep soaking tub, a telephone, and a television.

Executive Suites (mid $600 range) offer separate living rooms and bedrooms, bay windows, and two bathrooms with deep soaking tubs and separate showers.

Regardless of your choice of rooms, you'll be served by a "personal room attendant" who is at your beck and call day and night.

THE FACTS

*One hundred forty-one rooms, each with private bath.
Complimentary continental breakfast included. Restaurant
and lounge. Swimming pool and spa. Fitness center. Ten
tennis courts. Golf course. Day spa. Complimentary bicycle
rentals. Disabled access. Two-night minimum stay required
during weekends and holidays. Moderate to deluxe.*

GETTING THERE

*From Highway 101, take Lindero Canyon exit and drive
south on Lindero to Agoura Road. Turn right on Agoura
Drive and take first driveway on right, past golf course
to inn.*

WESTLAKE VILLAGE INN
31943 Agoura Road
Westlake Village, CA 91361
Telephone: (818) 889-0230
Web site: www.westlakevillageinn.com

Because of our California native status and innumerable romantic reconnaissance missions covering familiar ground, we sometimes feel like the travel honeymoon has finally ended. Then, just when we smugly conclude that we've seen it all, along comes an exciting new discovery to remind us that California is still a land of surprises.

With this revised edition of *Weekends for Two*, one of our favorite new finds is Westlake Village Inn, which we stumbled upon during an inland drive from the beach. Located about twenty miles north of Malibu across Highway 101 from Thousand Oaks, this delightful destination property offers convenient, romantic refuge from the more congested urban communities that sit just far enough away.

Occupying seventeen acres, the inn is set against Westlake Village Golf Course and a small lake. Accommodations are spread among a half-dozen or so buildings that face either the links or a pool and garden area. Couples who enjoy recreation and sports will particularly enjoy the array of activities here. In addition to golf, the inn offers several tennis courts and a fitness facility. Complimentary bike rentals are also available. Those preferring less strenuous activity will enjoy spending time together strolling the property's lush trellised walkways, rose arbor, and gardens, or simply hanging out in the comfortable guest rooms.

ROOMS FOR ROMANCE

For purposes of this book, we suggest couples on romantic holiday pass on the perfectly nice Courtyard and Lakeview Rooms (mid $100 range) and book a room that's slightly more expensive but much more conducive to an amorous adventure.

For example, the Executive Suites (high $100 range) are spacious corner units offering sitting areas and sofas. Business Suites (low $200 range) strike us as especially suited to the business of romance. These four-hundred-square-foot guest rooms are elegantly furnished and feature oversized bathrooms and fireplaces.

Spa tubs and fireplaces are the special romantic amenities found in the Mini Suites (low $200 range), while the Master Suites (mid $200 range) are among our favorites. These two-room units feature living and bedroom areas separated by a two-sided fireplace. The bathrooms have spa tubs, showers, and dual sinks.

For a splurge, the Deluxe Golf View Suites (around $400) pamper guests with wraparound patios overlooking the courtyard and the golf course. The inn also offers a spectacular accommodation called the Villa (around $900) whose features include a dining room, a living room, a spiral stairway, two fireplaces, a marble and granite bathroom with a spa tub for two, and a palatial bedroom fit for royalty.

THE FACTS

Eight cottages, each with private bath. Complimentary continental breakfast served on the patio or delivered to your room. Swimming pool and spa. Disabled access. Two-to-three-night minimum stay required during weekends; two-night minimum stay during holiday periods. Moderate to deluxe.

GETTING THERE

From Highway 101 at Ventura, take Highway 33 to Ojai. Drive ten miles to Highway 150 turnoff to Santa Barbara. Go straight at signal and drive a half-mile to Blue Iguana Inn (sister property) on right at corner of Loma Drive and Highway 33. Guests check in here and receive a map to nearby Emerald Iguana.

EMERALD IGUANA INN
Blanche Street
Ojai, CA 93023
Telephone: (805) 646-5277
Web site: www.emeraldiguana.com

Our first clue to the special nature of Emerald Iguana Inn came in the form of somewhat cryptic directions. In order to "preserve the tranquility" of its accommodations, Emerald Iguana asks its guests to check in at a nearby sister property where they're presented with a secret map to their cottage. Think of it as a treasure map to a delightfully unusual enclave of eclectic cottages. It's a perfect destination for couples looking for something a bit different and extraordinary.

Award-winning architect Marc Whitman designed the whimsical property, combining sculptural detail with artistic touches of stone, wood, and copper. Proprietor Julia Whitman furnished the rooms with antiques she handpicked in Indonesia.

ROOMS FOR ROMANCE

The eight cottages are offered with one, two, or even three bedrooms. If you're planning a romantic getaway for the two of you, a one-bedroom unit will do just fine. One of our favorites is Frog (upper $200 range), a storybook-style, stone-walled cottage with a covered furnished patio. Inside is an inviting living room with a gas stove and hardwood furniture including a couch and a chair, all under a vaulted and beamed ceiling. There's also a dining table and a kitchen. Upstairs is a cozy bedroom with an antique bed placed between two windows. The bathroom has a spa tub.

We also were impressed with Cricket (mid $200 range), which combines cozy indoor comforts with multiple outdoor living spaces. There's a private patio downstairs and two private balconies off the upstairs bedroom. The bathroom has a spa tub. There's a cozy downstairs living room and dining area as well as a kitchen.

Another good choice is the enchanting Treehouse (low $200 range), reached by stairs and offering a very romantic second-floor bedroom where a large window affords a great treetop view, either from the antique couch or the bed. Downstairs is a living room with a couch and chairs, a gas stove, and a full kitchen.

Among the amenities of Peacock (low $200 range) are Persian rugs, a woodburning stove, a clawfoot tub surrounded by an antique carved wooden screen, and a separate bathroom with a nicely tiled shower.

DAYTIME DIVERSIONS

Skiing is the popular winter pastime at Bear Mountain and Snow Summit near BIG BEAR LAKE and at Snow Valley and Green Valley Nordic Ski Area near RUNNING SPRINGS.

To see LAKE ARROWHEAD up close, hop aboard the paddlewheeler Arrowhead Queen, departing regularly from the marina, year-round. The Arrowhead Village swimming beach and marina are open during the late spring and summer. The village at Lake Arrowhead has more than two hundred specialty shops.

In BIG BEAR, Magic Mountain Recreation Area attracts summer visitors with its popular mountainside alpine slide. Big Bear Lake, eight miles long and one mile wide, is also a summer magnet with swimming, fishing, and sailing.

TABLES FOR TWO

Our LAKE ARROWHEAD innkeepers recommend Avanti's in SKY FOREST and Casual Elegance in BLUE JAY. Madlon's is a BIG BEAR favorite, while the North Shore Cafe in nearby FAWNSKIN is also recommended.

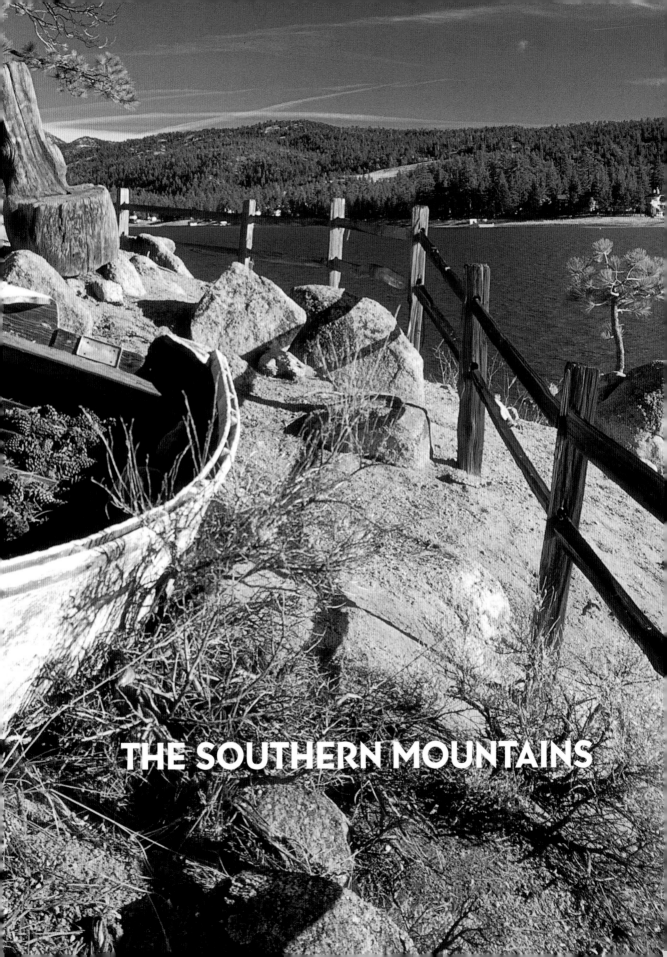

THE SOUTHERN MOUNTAINS

THE FACTS

Eight rooms, each with private bath and gas fireplace; six with tubs for two. Complimentary full breakfast served at tables for two or more. Complimentary wine and refreshments and after-dinner dessert and liqueurs. Disabled access. Two-night minimum stay required during weekends and holiday periods. Moderate to expensive.

GETTING THERE

Big Bear Lake is approximately two hours from Los Angeles and five hours from San Diego. From Interstate 10 in San Bernardino, take Highway 30 exit and travel five miles. Exit on Highway 330, which becomes Highway 18 in Running Springs. In Big Bear Lake Village turn left on Pine Knot Road, right on Big Bear Boulevard, and right on Knight Avenue. Follow to inn on left.

For a destination resort community whose weekend population can swell to a hundred thousand, Big Bear Lake has historically lacked a corresponding selection of romantic getaway destinations. Because overnight accommodations have tended more toward anonymous motels and homes-turned-inns, traveling romantics have had few options. Fortunately, things are looking up, thanks to the recent opening of Alpenhorn Bed and Breakfast, in our opinion Big Bear's most romantic destination.

With its wildflower gardens, tall pines, wooden balconies, and stone fireplaces, the eight-room Alpenhorn might best be described as an impressive boutique mountain lodge. Open only since the turn of the new century, the inn presides over two acres of alpine forest set between the village and Snow Summit ski area. It's an especially convenient location for a Big Bear ski getaway with a romantic twist.

Two streams meander through the grounds, which are profuse with pine and fruit trees, bushes, and flowers. Inside, a large two-sided brick fireplace separates the cozy parlor and the dining room. There's also a video library stocked with Academy Award–winning movies, but our guess is that the two of you will opt to create your own in-room entertainment—without Oscar.

ROOMS FOR ROMANCE

At the high end of the rate and romance scale is the Alpenrose (upper $200 range), a spacious first-floor hideaway with a private balcony, a marble fireplace, a king-sized iron-canopied bed, a large and luxurious bathroom with a spa tub for two and a separate shower. There's also a bay-windowed sitting area with a couch and two matching chairs.

Similarly priced is the Bellflower, also on the first floor and boasting a private, garden-view balcony, a brick fireplace, and a bathroom with a two-headed shower and a whirlpool tub for two. The two twin beds convert to a comfy king-sized bed.

Also recommended are the smaller Edelweiss, Rosebay, Primrose, and Amarella Rooms, which are offered in the mid $200 range and feature queen-sized beds, spa tubs big enough for two along with separate showers, and private balconies.

ALPENHORN BED AND BREAKFAST
601 Knight Avenue (P.O. Box 2912)
Big Bear Lake, CA 92315
Telephone: (909) 866-5700;
toll-free: (888) 829-6600
Web site:www.alpenhorn.com

THE FACTS

Five rooms, each with private bath, fireplace, refrigerator, and DVD player. Complimentary full breakfast served on the deck or delivered to certain guest rooms. Complimentary afternoon refreshments. No disabled access. Two-night minimum stay required during weekends; three-night minimum stay during holiday periods. Moderate to deluxe.

GETTING THERE

From Interstate 10, take Highway 30/330, then follow Highway 330 to Running Springs where it becomes Highway 18. Follow Highway 18 to Big Bear Dam. Veer toward left at dam and follow Highway 38 (North Shore Drive) for two miles to inn.

WINDY POINT INN
39015 North Shore Drive (P.O. Box 375)
Fawnskin, CA 92333
Telephone: (909) 866-2746
Web site: www.windypointinn.com

WINDY POINT INN

There's nothing like a view of a beautiful mountain lake to ignite romantic sparks, and we're not aware of a better place from which to savor the panorama of Big Bear Lake than Windy Point Inn, located on the lake's quiet north shore.

The inn, which passersby might easily mistake for a large mountain home, is set among pines on a breezy, private peninsula just steps from the water's edge. Two sandy beaches are close by.

Built in 1990, the chalet-style inn contains five bedrooms. Each is equipped with its own bathroom and woodburning fireplace. The downstairs common area has a sunken lake-view living room with a corner woodburning stove. A grand piano sits nearby on a polished hardwood floor.

ROOMS FOR ROMANCE

Since our last visit, proprietors Val and Kent Kessler have created two fabulous new suites. The Coves is a skylit upper corner room with an awe-inspiring lake view that can be enjoyed not only from the couch and the deck, but from the privacy of the in-room whirlpool tub set adjacent to the bed. Outfitted with similar features is The Shores, set at lake level and lulling guests with the sound of water lapping against the rocks. Both of these rooms (mid $200 range) are also equipped with fireplaces.

Another ultra-romantic choice is The Peaks (mid $200 range), an impressive corner hideaway with a terrific lake view that's visible from every window. A large wraparound sofa sits in front of the fireplace, and the king-sized bed is situated under a skylight for star gazing. For lake gazing there's a private deck as well as a lake-view spa tub for two. Completing the picture is a combination steam-and-stall shower for two.

The Pines (upper $100 range) is a split-level affair. In one area is a queen-sized bed and a corner fireplace facing your toes. You'll step up to the sitting area with a wraparound sofa, a skylit spa tub for two, and a window seat offering a lake view.

Also popular is The Sands (mid $100 range), which makes up for its comparatively small size with a grand view of the lake. This cozy room also features a fireplace.

THE FACTS

Four rooms, each with private bath and videocassette player; two with fireplaces; three with spa tubs. Full breakfast served at large communal table or on lake-view balcony. Complimentary evening wine and cheese and desserts. Complimentary beverages and snacks available daily. No disabled access. Two-night minimum stay required during the summer and holiday periods. Moderate to deluxe.

GETTING THERE

From San Bernardino, take Highway 18 to Lake Arrowhead. At signal, turn right on Highway 173 and drive three miles to Hospital Road. Turn right; inn is first house on right.

Just before wrapping up our south-state romantic inn-vestigations, we were fortunate to hear about Chateau du Lac, among the newer inns at Lake Arrowhead, allegedly a paradise for lovers. A lucky break. As it turned out, the chateau emerged as one of the most romantic retreats in the southern mountains.

When innkeepers Oscar and Jody Wilson happened by here in the late 1980s, the structure was being built as a house. The Wilsons took over, made some modifications, and finished it as an elegant mountain inn.

A beautifully eclectic mix of styles employing clapboard, stone, brick, and artful white trim, Chateau du Lac occupies a heavenly spot on the lake, opposite the village, whose distant lights twinkle at night. New owners had redecorated the rooms at around the time of our most recent travels.

ROOMS FOR ROMANCE

The Loft (around $200) is a comfortable suite containing a sitting room with a couch and a private entrance for discreet comings and goings. You'll also appreciate the fireplace and a spa tub that will accommodate two in a pinch.

On the uppermost level of the inn is The Room at the Top of the Stairs (mid $100 range), an intimate suite with a television, a cozy attic sitting room, and a spa tub (high $100 range).

The Lake View Suite (low to mid $200 range) is a seductive showplace. Below the open-beam vaulted ceiling is a brick fireplace, nicely papered walls, a stereo system, and a spa tub for two set in a windowed alcove. There's also a balcony overlooking the lake.

The views of the lake from this and other of the chateau's rooms will blow your socks off, along with a few other garments.

CHATEAU DU LAC

911 Hospital Road/Highway 173
(P.O. Box 1098)
Lake Arrowhead, CA 92352
Telephone: (909) 337-6488;
toll-free: (800) 601-8722
Web site: www.chateau-du-lac.com

DAYTIME DIVERSIONS

In the Southern California desert, daytime activities are somewhat seasonal. During the winter months, when the weather is often in the comfortable 70-degree range, visitors head for the golf courses, tennis courts, or shopping in downtown PALM SPRINGS or at El Paseo in PALM DESERT.

In the summertime, when the mercury pushes the century-plus mark, the downtown cafes turn on their misting machines and the resort pools teem with guests seeking relief from the heat.

One year-round activity that shouldn't be missed is a trip up the Palm Springs Aerial Tramway to a cool elevation of 8,500 feet. The tram entrance is on Highway 111 and Tramway Road.

Other popular destinations are Joshua Tree National Park outside TWENTYNINE PALMS and Anza-Borrego Park. These parks are especially romantic during the winter months when daytime temperatures are mild and the desert flowers are in full bloom.

TABLES FOR TWO

Our PALM SPRINGS innkeepers recommend Le Vallauxis and St. James at the Vineyard. In DESERT HOT SPRINGS, try Palm Korea, South of the Border, or the more upscale Italian steakhouse called Capri. Cuistot, Doug Arango's, and Sullivan's Steakhouse, all in PALM DESERT, have highly recommended pairings of food and wine.

THE DESERT

THE FACTS

Eight rooms, each with private bath; most with tubs for two and gas fireplaces. Complimentary full breakfast served at tables for two or delivered to your room. Complimentary evening wine and refreshments. Swimming pool and spa. Disabled access. Two-night minimum stay required during weekends; three-night minimum stay during holiday periods. Expensive to deluxe.

GETTING THERE

From Interstate 10, merge onto Highway 111 south toward Palm Springs. Take North Palm Canyon Drive into Palm Springs and follow to Tahquitz Canyon Way. Turn right and follow to inn on right.

THE WILLOWS HISTORIC PALM SPRINGS INN

412 West Tahquitz Canyon Way
(P.O. Box 3340)
Palm Springs, CA 92263
Telephone: (760) 320-0771;
toll-free: (800) 966-9597
Web site: www.thewillowspalmsprings.com

THE WILLOWS HISTORIC PALM SPRINGS INN

Designed and built during the Roaring Twenties as the winter home of wealthy New York attorney Samuel Untermyer, The Willows played host over the years to such luminaries as Albert Einstein, Clark Gable, Carole Lombard, Shirley Temple, and Marion Davies. These days, while the guest book may list less famous names, the property hasn't lost any of its luster. In fact, The Willows is one of Palm Springs' most exclusive and romantic overnight hideaways.

Describing the property as restored is an understatement. With its private bathrooms, entertainment centers, and data ports, The Willows of today pampers guests like you and I with comforts that visitors of yesteryear couldn't have imagined.

Among the inn's many notable features are its hillside gardens and dramatic desert vistas. It's also famous for the waterfall that plunges down the mountainside just outside the inn's garden breakfast room.

ROOMS FOR ROMANCE

You'll need to make multiple visits to experience the inn's variety of accommodations, which range from dark and masculine to frilly and feminine. The most expensive is the Marion Davies Room (upper $500 range), named after the Hollywood actress and mistress of publishing tycoon William Randolph Hearst. This room has a balcony with a view, a handsome fireplace, a king-sized carved wooden bed, and a romantic sitting area with a couch. The bathroom features a clawfoot tub big enough for two, set under a silver chandelier against a window with a garden view.

Offered in the mid $500 range, the Library served as a honeymoon retreat for Gable and Lombard. This room has an impressive carved and coffered wooden ceiling, two sturdy leather chairs facing an ornate desk, a veranda that looks onto a private garden patio, and private entrances. The bathroom holds a bathtub and a separate shower.

The Waterfall Room (mid $400 range), furnished with warm, blond-toned bird's-eye maple dressers and a queen-sized sleigh bed, features a dramatic view of the waterfall and mountains.

Water from the shower splashes onto a large boulder in the unusual bathroom of the aptly named Rock Room (around $500). On the other side of the rock sits a tub for two. In addition to a sitting room, this hideaway has a private mountain-view balcony above the swimming pool.

Albert Einstein spent many nights in his namesake room (around $500), which features art deco–style mahogany furniture and a private garden patio adjacent to the waterfall.

THE FACTS

Eight villas, each with bedroom, kitchen, living/dining rooms, fireplace, bathroom with shower and spa tub, and private outdoor patio; most with private outdoor whirlpool tubs for two and fire pits. Complimentary breakfast served anywhere on the property. Complimentary afternoon tea. Swimming pool. Disabled access. Two-night minimum stay required during weekends and some holiday periods. Deluxe.

GETTING THERE

From Interstate 10, merge onto Highway 111 south toward Palm Springs. Take North Palm Canyon Drive and follow past Tahquitz Canyon Way to West Arenas Road. Turn right and follow to inn on right between Lugo and Patencio Roads.

ANDALUSIAN COURT BED AND BREAKFAST
458 West Arenas Road
Palm Springs, CA 92262
Telephone: (760) 323-9980;
toll-free: (888) 947-6667
Web site: www.andalusiancourt.com

Whenever we hear about a new property created by a husband-and-wife team, we're among the first to visit. In our experience, some of the most fabulous getaway destinations are those inspired and designed by happy couples whose combined romantic visions yield wonderfully romantic results. The Andalusian Court is no exception. Conceived by inveterate travelers Dave and Trudy Johnston, this newly refurbished enclave of private casitas tops our list of the desert's most romantic destinations.

The Johnstons, along with a cadre of artisans, spent two years reviving a tired 1920s-era inn to create an enchanting Moorish-style villa with lovely gardens, enchanted pathways, and inspired outdoor architecture, not to mention the delightfully decadent and eclectic casitas, all framed by the dramatic San Jacinto Mountains.

While such an endeavor would have strained some relationships, the Johnstons were sufficiently inspired to start their own hospitality business with additional new properties including El Pedragal, a small, foothill villa resort that opened in 2003.

ROOMS FOR ROMANCE

Each of the eight casitas is essentially a self-contained home away from home. With a couple of bags of groceries, the two of you could easily disappear here for days without opening your door to the outside world.

Evoking the Spanish Revival and Arts and Crafts periods, the uniquely styled casitas (low to mid $400 range) are artful, spacious, warm, and comfortable. All feature central air conditioning and heating, separate fully equipped kitchens, living rooms, bedrooms, and bathrooms, as well as private outdoor patios. Most have romantic outdoor spa tubs for two and fire pits.

One of our favorites is Villa 2, resplendent with stone floors, stone fireplace, and whimsical stone accents in the bathroom. The stone-walled and stained-glass-windowed shower and bedroom with beamed cathedral ceiling and canopied bed are particularly romantic. This villa also has an outdoor tub for two.

The romantic, lamp-lit bedroom in Villa 6 caught our eye, as did the raised, two-sided fireplace that warms Villa 4. Both of these accommodations have outdoor tubs.

Those who venture away from their casitas during the daytime hours typically head for the courtyard swimming pool, while the illuminated cobbled pathways, outdoor art, and meditation garden are especially magical at night.

THE FACTS

Thirty-one rooms, suites, and villas, several with fireplaces, patio, and fully equipped kitchens. Complimentary continental breakfast served poolside or in your room. Restaurant. Two swimming pools, one spa, and bar. Complimentary morning newspaper. Disabled access. Smoking is allowed. Two-night minimum stay during weekends; three-night minimum stay during holiday periods. Moderate to deluxe.

GETTING THERE

From Interstate 10, exit Highway 111 (Palms Springs) to center of town. Veer left at downward split in road onto East Palm Canyon Drive. Turn left on Indian Trail and follow to inn.

Although dozens and dozens of hotels and motels line the main thoroughfares from one end of Palm Springs to the other, we found the real gems only by poking around the side streets. Among these hidden treasures is Villa Royale, one of Palm Springs' best-kept secrets.

From its early days as a 1930s-era private home, the property has grown to thirty-one antique-furnished guest rooms and two swimming pools spread over more than three lushly landscaped acres. Since our last visit, the property has undergone yet another renovation.

ROOMS FOR ROMANCE

The tile-roofed guest wings are situated around a series of courtyards framed by pillars, arches, shade trees, potted plants, and cascading bougainvillea.

For the most privacy, we suggest rooms 201 through 204. These face a quiet fountain courtyard well removed from the public areas. Room 203 (mid $200 range), a one-bedroom corner suite facing a fountain courtyard, features a French theme with a king-sized bed and a fireplace. The bath is reached via a pretty leaded-glass door. The suite is equipped with a small dining room and an intimate kitchen. At another corner of the courtyard is room 201, an oft-requested retreat (mid $200 range).

The inn's most remote accommodations, rooms 301 through 309, face the swimming pool farthest from the dining room and the office.

One of the inn's largest and most unusual rooms is 305 (mid $200 range), decorated with a trove of antique items. Two facing love seats sit before a large brick fireplace. A beamed cathedral ceiling runs the length of the room, from the king-sized bed to a small serving bar, next to a spacious kitchen. The private patio is shaded by an olive tree.

VILLA ROYALE
1620 Indian Trail
Palm Springs, CA 92264
Telephone: (760) 327-2314;
toll-free: (800) 245-2314
Web site: www.villaroyale.com

THE FACTS
Ten rooms, each with private bath. Complimentary continental breakfast served at large communal table. Lunch available at extra charge. Swimming pool and spa. Spa treatments available. No disabled access. Two-night minimum stay required from Thursday through Sunday. Moderate.

GETTING THERE
From Interstate 10, take Palm Drive exit and drive north for five miles to Hacienda. Turn right and drive one mile to stop sign. Go past stop sign and make first left. Hotel is about eight miles from Palm Springs Airport.

HOPE SPRINGS
68075 Club Circle Drive
Desert Hot Springs, CA 92240
Telephone: (760) 329-4003
Web site: www.hopespringsresort.com

It's almost as if this formerly forlorn and neglected little gem, which endured not only a relentless desert sun but also a succession of some twenty different owners, was patiently hanging on, hoping to one day find its niche. Well, hope springs eternal. Today, this intriguing property is enjoying new life as a minimalist, aesthetic oasis high above the Coachella Valley.

Although it was built in 1958, Hope Springs' current incarnation dates back to only 2000. That's when Hollywood graphic designers Steve Samiof and Mick Haggerty reopened the place after extensive renovations, much of them undertaken by the owners themselves without the aid of detailed plans or blueprints. The result is a property that has been praised by architects and heralded by fans of minimalism.

ROOMS FOR ROMANCE

Hope Springs is a destination for couples who truly enjoy desert solitude, not to mention each other's company, and those who don't require traditional hotel amenities, room service, or plush furnishings. Rooms are as sparse as any we've ever seen, furnished with not much more than platform-mounted king-sized beds, Japanese paper lamps, CD players, and a period-inspired chair or two. Floors are polished concrete. Bathrooms are lean and clean as well, featuring simple green-painted cabinetry and chrome accents. One critic described Hope Springs as "a total head cleanser."

Also bedecked with period furnishings from yard sales, the outdoor living areas are more typical of desert resorts in the region. Rooms face a wonderful courtyard whose centerpieces are three spring-fed swimming pools boasting varying temperatures from 90 to 105 degrees. Palm trees and cacti surround the patio areas. Although there's no restaurant on site, the hotel serves up lunches and smoothies for an extra charge.

The high-season (winter) rate for a standard room at Hope Springs is in the mid $100 range. Four rooms have kitchenettes equipped with a sink, a microwave oven, a small refrigerator, and a small table and chairs. These are offered in the high $100 range.

THE FACTS

Twenty-four rooms, each with private bath; many with kitchenettes and gas stoves. Complimentary continental breakfast served at communal table or delivered to your room. Complimentary afternoon refreshments. Swimming pool and spa. Health club privileges. Spa treatments. Disabled access. Two-night minimum stay required during weekends; two-to-three-night minimum stay during holiday periods. Moderate to expensive.

GETTING THERE

From Interstate 10, take Monterey Street exit and drive south on Monterey Street for six miles. Cross over Highway 111 and take first left onto El Paseo. Drive five blocks and turn right onto San Luis Rey. Drive one block to hotel on left at corner of Shadow Mountain Drive.

The kitschy style of the 1940s is not only preserved but celebrated at this desert classic. From its low-slung architecture and spindly palms to the in-room goodie baskets bulging with treats from the past like Nehi soda and Necco wafer candies, Mojave provides a tantalizing taste of midcentury resort life—desert style.

Enjoying a great location just steps from Palm Desert's lively El Paseo shopping district, this little oasis reopened as Mojave shortly after the turn of the new century following an extensive refurbishing that played off of the property's retro roots. Operated by the same company that created Santa Barbara's Inn of the Spanish Garden (see separate listing), Mojave was nursed back to life by a San Francisco design firm that specializes in the historic renovation of landmark hotels. The results are evident upon entering the lobby with its sea grass carpeting and vintage desert black-and-white photography.

ROOMS FOR ROMANCE

Although the guest rooms evoke the proper period atmosphere, we doubt the property's original furnishings were quite this comfortable. Reproduction French Moderne armchairs and occasional tables along with custom bleached oak furniture fill the rooms and suites these days. Rooms feature video-cassette and CD players. Vintage movies and musical selections complete the theme.

The desert's high season runs from January through May, and rates at Mojave during this period start in the mid $100 range for a standard guest room and climb to around $200 for a larger suite. Rooms are a relative bargain during the sweltering summer months, with rates topping out in the low $100 range. Some rooms feature gas stoves, fireplaces, and classic kitchenettes. Each of Mojave's two dozen rooms has a private patio. Many of the rooms face a courtyard lush with citrus and palm trees, as well as lawn areas. There's a swimming pool and spa and a cabana where guests are pampered with spa treatments. In-room spa services are also available.

MOJAVE

73721 Shadow Mountain Drive
Palm Desert, CA 92260
Telephone: (760) 346-6121;
toll-free: (800) 391-1104
Web site: www.hotelmojave.com

DAYTIME DIVERSIONS

Two of SAN DIEGO'S most popular attractions are within walking distance of the Horton Grand Hotel, our featured downtown destination. Horton Plaza is a multilevel shopping center on Island Avenue, located between Third and Fourth Avenues.

Seaport Village, a rambling shopping and restaurant complex with a great water-view sidewalk, is a great place to while away an afternoon.

Old Town State Historic Park, home of our other featured San Diego inn, offers a glimpse of early San Diego as well as the Bazaar del Mundo shopping plaza and wildly popular Mexican restaurants.

Boutiques, upscale stores, and restaurants are the main attractions of exclusive and enchanting LA JOLLA, whose downtown village is set against a Pacific Ocean backdrop.

TABLES FOR TWO

SAN DIEGO restaurants worthy of note include Cafe Pacifica, Dakota Grill and Spirits, Greystone Steakhouse, Fleming's Prime Steakhouse, and Laurel Restaurant. In Old Town, Casa de Pico and Casa de Bandini are top Mexican restaurant choices.

In LA JOLLA, we can recommend Donovan's, A. R. Valentien, George's at the Cove, Nine-Ten, Sante Ristorante, Top O' the Cove, and Tapenade.

Mille Fleurs and Rancho Valencia Restaurant are our top choices in RANCHO SANTA FE. In BORREGO SPRINGS, we recommend Butterfield at La Casa del Zorro, one of our featured destinations. The casual Carlee's Place is a favorite among Borrego Springs locals.

THE SAN DIEGO AREA

THE FACTS

Eight rooms and suites, each with private bath and gas fireplace. Complimentary full breakfast may be taken to your room. Beach access two hundred yards away. Disabled access. Courtesy guest pickup at nearby Amtrak train station. Two-night minimum stay required during weekends and holiday periods. Moderate to expensive.

GETTING THERE

From Interstate 5, exit at Carlsbad Village Drive. Turn left on Carlsbad Boulevard and left on Walnut Avenue.

PELICAN COVE INN

A century ago, Carlsbad earned a fair amount of fame after the accidental discovery of curative water under the village. In recent years, however, the spotlight has drifted away from this quaint little burg, shining more brightly on the trendy streets of nearby La Jolla.

Weekending San Diegans and others who have been lucky enough to discover Carlsbad's Pelican Cove Inn would probably prefer that we kept this romantic destination to ourselves. But we couldn't resist.

This charming inn, situated just two blocks from the beach and a short stroll from the village, was crafted in 1987 from a couple of little apartment complexes. Since then it has more than doubled in size and now boasts an adjacent two-story unit that houses four large rooms.

ROOMS FOR ROMANCE

From the street, the most eye-catching feature of the light-blue inn is an octagonal wing, the bottom level of which serves as the public room. On the second story is the intimate Newport Room (low to mid $100 range), where a queen-sized brass feather bed sits under the windowed octagonal dome.

A high king-sized captain's bed made of dark wood dominates the skylit Carlsbad Room (mid $100 range).

Most coveted among visiting romantics are the Coronado and La Jolla Rooms (high $100 range). Coronado has a king-sized draped, four-poster bed. The bathroom holds a spa tub for two. This first-floor room is decorated in hues of peach and sea-foam green.

La Jolla, styled in black and champagne tones, boasts a high, rounded ceiling and expansive windows. In the bathroom is a spa tub for two.

For guests who can't bear to leave the inn on a nice day, the owners have created a sundeck atop the second floor.

PELICAN COVE INN
320 Walnut Avenue
Carlsbad, CA 92008
Telephone: (619) 434-5995
Web site: www.pelican-cove.com

THE FACTS

Sixteen rooms, each with private bath. Complimentary full gourmet breakfast served in the garden. No disabled access. Two-night minimum stay required during weekends. Moderate to deluxe.

GETTING THERE

Take Interstate 5, exit at La Jolla Village Drive west. Turn left on Torrey Pines Road, right on Prospect Place through town to Draper Avenue. Inn sits between La Jolla Presbyterian Church and Women's Club.

THE BED-AND-BREAKFAST INN AT LA JOLLA

We made a special point of visiting the Bed-and-Breakfast Inn at La Jolla on an early midweek afternoon. It was the only time we could peek into multiple rooms since the inn is so solidly booked during weekends.

The hardwood squeaked underfoot as we explored the hallways of this early-1900s cubist mansion, home for a time to the family of composer John Philip Sousa. Ten rooms are located in the main house. Six have been added in a newer adjoining building.

ROOMS FOR ROMANCE

Holiday (mid $300 range), a large corner room, has a draped, canopied four-poster bed that sits before a fireplace. There's also a separate sitting area and a private bath with a tub for two. Although this room is located just off the front entry area, it is one of our romantic favorites.

Our highest recommendation goes to the Irving Gill Penthouse (around $400), a luxury suite on the second floor with a library sitting room, a king-sized bed, and a tub for two. One of the most memorable features is the deck from which to enjoy ocean views and sunsets.

Among the most affordable is Peacock Salon (mid $200 range), a bright second-floor room with a queen-sized bed, a small bathroom with a tub-and-shower combination, and a tiny balcony overlooking the garden.

Country Village (low to mid $200 range) is a spacious room with a sitting area but no view to speak of.

For those yearning to see the ocean, Pacific View (high $200 range) offers the best view in the house, along with a sitting room and a fireplace. Other rooms have nice views that might include the ocean and/or the gardens. Some rooms do not have inspiring views. If views are important to the two of you, be sure to inquire about them when making a reservation.

THE BED-AND-BREAKFAST INN AT LA JOLLA
7753 Draper Avenue
La Jolla, CA 92037
Telephone: (619) 456-2066
Web site: ww.innlajolla.com

THE FACTS

Twenty suites, each with private bath and refrigerator with complimentary refreshments. Complimentary continental breakfast served in lobby or delivered to your room. Fitness center. In-room spa services. Complimentary underground parking. Disabled access. Two-night minimum stay required during weekends and holiday periods. Deluxe.

GETTING THERE

From north, exit Interstate 5 at La Jolla Village Drive exit. Turn right on La Jolla Village Drive, left on Torrey Pines Road, and right on Prospect Place. Follow to hotel at corner of Prospect and Herschel. From south, exit Interstate 5 at Ardath Road exit. Turn left on Torrey Pines and right on Prospect Place.

HOTEL PARISI
1111 Prospect Place
La Jolla, CA 92037
Telephone: (858) 454-1511
Web site: www.hotelparisi.com

Our romantic sojourns have taken us to some delightfully distinctive destinations, but nowhere have we found a place quite like Hotel Parisi, whose staff includes a yoga instructor, an acupuncturist, and a massage therapist and where guest-room phones have a direct connection to the office of an on-call clinical psychologist. This Mediterranean-style "urban boutique retreat," located near the ocean at the exclusive heart of La Jolla, is an artful and calming mix of east and west; old age and new age. Hints of Northern Italy, Czech Republic, and Asia are blended with feng shui with an eye toward creating what designer Stephanie Parisi Walters describes as "magical places that soothe the senses and relax the mind." For traveling romantics, it's the perfect prescription for a memorable getaway.

After a day exploring the bustling shops of La Jolla, Hotel Parisi is great place to relax and unwind. Set behind a palm-fronted, Italian facade, this small hotel, a favorite among A-list celebrities, sets a meditative mood from the moment you enter the doors. The impressive lobby, with a fireplace and a fountain, offers a taste of what awaits behind your guest room door.

ROOMS FOR ROMANCE

Lacking dramatic white water ocean views and typical hotel amenities like a swimming pool or a restaurant, Hotel Parisi lavishes loads of attention on its guest suites, the smallest of which measure more than four hundred generous square feet in size.

The comfy furnishings are custom made, and the beds are cloudlike, with duvets, pillows, and upscale linens. Each suite also features track lighting, an entertainment center, a walk-out balcony, an ergonomically styled desk, a table and chairs, and a refrigerator stocked with complimentary refreshments. Room service is also available.

Bathrooms are destinations unto themselves and feature large showers with dual showerheads, bathtubs for one with contoured backrests, and custom-made, all-natural bath products. A long impressive menu of in-room spa services can be ordered with a simple phone call.

Standard suites, which feature all the above-mentioned amenities but do not offer views, are offered for around $300, many of these have nice sitting areas. Those with the choicest ocean views carry tariffs in the low $400 range. Rooms 12, 14, and 15, for example, offer ocean views beyond the village roofs. The rate for a suite with a partial ocean view is in the upper $300 range.

THE FACTS

Ten rooms, each with private bath. Amenities include bathrobes and fresh flowers. Complimentary full breakfast served at communal table. Disabled access. Two-night minimum stay required during weekends and holiday periods. Moderate to expensive.

GETTING THERE

From Interstate 5, take Old Town Avenue exit. Turn left on San Diego Avenue and right on Harney Street into Heritage Park.

HERITAGE PARK INN
2470 Heritage Park Row
San Diego, CA 92110
Telephone: (619) 299-6832;
toll-free: (800) 995-2470
Web site: www.heritageparkinn.com

HERITAGE PARK INN

Old Town San Diego's most charming overnight destination is the centerpiece of Heritage Park Victorian Village, a historic enclave of nineteenth-century structures set within an eight-acre county park dedicated to Victorian preservation. Located within a short stroll of Old Town historic sites, shops, and eateries, Heritage Park Inn is a romantic and enchanting slice of California history.

Proud and picture-perfect on the outside, the inn consists of two grand period homes, each boasting a charming interior that elegantly reflects the golden age. Throughout the public rooms and guest chambers are beautiful settees, chairs, and lamps that date from the 1800s. Even the carpets feature antique patterns.

ROOMS FOR ROMANCE

Most requested is the Drawing Room (low $200 range), located in the adjacent refurbished Victorian next door. A sunny bay window illuminates this room furnished with a queen-sized bed, a trundle daybed, an armoire hiding a small refrigerator and a videocassette player, and an in-room spa tub for two. The bathroom has a shower and an old-fashioned sink.

The spacious Manor Suite (mid $200 range), also located in the adjacent manse next door, has everything your romantic heart could desire. A private parlor holds an ornamental fireplace, videocassette player, and stereo, while the master bedroom holds a king-sized four-poster bed and a hundred-year-old fainting couch. The spacious bathroom has a shower and a spa tub.

Another favorite is the Grandview Room (around $200), which spoils guests with a queen-sized canopied bed, a bay window with a fantastic view, and an old-fashioned oversized tub-turned-spa big enough for two.

The Forget-Me-Not Room (upper $100 range) won a Waverly design award for its elegant Victorian appointments. The room has a decorative fireplace, a stenciled ceiling, and a private bath with a clawfoot tub and a shower. The beautiful dark sleigh bed is framed by luscious draperies that are swagged from a crown.

The Garret (mid $100 range) is a third-floor hideaway with a harbor view, and the Victorian Rose (mid $100 range) faces the inn's pretty rose garden. Both of these rooms have private bathrooms with showers.

Guests should understand that while all of the rooms have their own bathrooms, some are detached from the rooms.

At the time of our visit, the inn offered sunset gondola cruises through the canals and waterways of Coronado. Maybe best of all, inn guests get preferential seating at one of Old Town's most popular Mexican restaurants.

HORTON GRAND HOTEL

311 Island Avenue

San Diego, CA 92101

Telephone: (619) 544-1886

Web site: www.hortongrand.com

THE FACTS

One hundred eight rooms, twenty-four suites, each with private bath, gas fireplace, television, phone, and air conditioning. Restaurant and bar. Honeymoon packages, including horse-drawn carriage ride available. Disabled access. Smoking is allowed in certain rooms. Moderate to deluxe.

GETTING THERE

Horton Grand is located two blocks from Horton Plaza shopping center on Island Avenue, between Third and Fourth Avenues. From San Diego Freeway (northbound), exit at Sixth Avenue and drive to Fourth Avenue. Turn left on Fourth, and right on Island. From San Diego Freeway (southbound), exit at Front Avenue and drive to Market. Turn left on Market, right on Fourth, and right on Island. Seaport Village shops and San Diego Convention Center are a short walk away.

HORTON GRAND HOTEL

We've heard of the earth moving during a romantic encounter, but the walls shaking and pictures turning? Some claim it has happened at the Horton Grand Hotel, but not necessarily during the heat of passion. The strange goings-on in room 309 are reportedly the works of a mischievous ghost named Roger, who makes his presence known from time to time.

Since its opening more than a hundred years ago, the venerable Horton Grand has come a long way. A couple of blocks, to be precise. It once stood on the site of San Diego's famous Horton Plaza and was moved, in thousands of pieces, down the street by forward-thinking developers bent on preserving a slice of San Diego history.

The resurrected structure is actually two hotels in one; the Horton Grand and the Kahle Saddlery Hotel, another century-old hostelry that likewise had been targeted for demolition.

The Horton Grand is a lovers' oasis in the heart of San Diego's Gaslamp Quarter. Its cowboy Victorian decor has given way to antiques, platformed and draped beds, lace curtains, and cozy gas fireplaces with marble mantels.

ROOMS FOR ROMANCE

While the hotel's rooms inspire romance, the street views don't. Our advice is to request one of the nicer third- or fourth-floor Balcony Courtyard Rooms facing the lovely interior brick courtyard (upper $100 range). The white wrought-iron balconies and mature shade trees are reminiscent of New Orleans' French Quarter. Some of our readers have reported, however, that occasional private courtyard parties can be a bit noisy.

The Horton Grand also has two dozen suites, each with antiques, two telephones, two televisions, a wet bar, a refrigerator, and a microwave. Furnishings and decor could benefit from some updating. We've also received reports of spotty housekeeping.

In each of the Horton Grand's accommodations, you'll find platformed queen-sized beds, ceiling fans, and guest books with descriptions of the romantic liaisons of former guests. Although some are candid enough to make a San Diego sailor blush, most of the diary entries are innocent, heart-felt reflections about rediscovering romance or savoring a long overdue getaway from the daily grind.

THE FACTS

Forty-nine suites, each with private bath, fireplace, tub for two, two televisions, and telephone. Amenities include fresh flowers and bathrobes. Fresh orange juice and newspaper delivered to your room each morning. Swimming pool and spa. Fitness center. Tennis courts. Croquet course. Guests have golf privileges at a nearby course. Disabled access. Smoking is allowed. Two-night minimum stay required during weekends; three-night minimum stay during summers and holiday weekends. Deluxe.

GETTING THERE

From Interstate 5, take Via de la Valle exit and drive east. Turn right on El Camino Real and drive for a half mile. Turn left on San Dieguito and drive for three miles. Turn right on Rancho Diegueno Road, and then make an immediate left on Rancho Valencia Road. Then turn left on Rancho Valencia Drive.

RANCHO VALENCIA RESORT

It's hard to believe this remote hilltop resort is only twenty-five minutes from bustling downtown San Diego. The madding crowd might as well be a million miles away. Situated above a quiet, upscale suburb of equestrian estates, the resort was planned for those who seek privacy. The public areas are well distanced from most suites and rooms, so you won't encounter other guests unless you want to. No wonder the guest list has included luminaries like Bill Clinton, Bill Gates, and Michael Jordan.

ROOMS FOR ROMANCE

The resort consists of twenty-six tile-roofed casitas housing forty-nine of the southland's most sumptuous suites. These privately situated units have beautifully landscaped patios dotted with striking blue umbrellas.

The Del Mar Suites, at more than eight hundred square feet, are the smallest and least expensive of the resort's accommodations. And they're all you need for a memorable romantic getaway. These have beamed ceilings, sunken living rooms with fireplaces, and expanses of windows with plantation shutters and French doors that open to private patios. You'll step up to the bedroom area with either a king-sized bed or two queen-sized beds. Tariffs for these rooms range from the mid $400 range to around $600 depending on location. Sunset-view rooms are the most expensive.

Budget permitting, the two of you will definitely enjoy the decadent new Grove Suites (from the low $700 range), which have private patio spas and steam showers with oversized rain showerheads.

RANCHO VALENCIA RESORT
5921 Valencia Circle (P.O. Box 9126)
Rancho Santa Fe, CA 92067
Telephone: (858) 756-1123
Web site: www.ranchovalencia.com

THE FACTS

Eighty rooms, each with private bath, telephone, and television; many have fireplaces; many have wet bars, kitchenettes, and/or private patios. Restaurant. Room service. Swimming pool, spa, English croquet course. Fitness center. Tennis courts with on-site pro. Guest privileges at several nearby golf courses. Disabled access. Two-night minimum stay required during some weekends; three-night minimum stay required during some weekends and during some holiday periods. Moderate to deluxe.

GETTING THERE

From Interstate 5 (San Diego Freeway), take Lomas Santa Fe Drive (S-8) exit. Inn is located approximately four miles east on this road. From Interstate 15, exit at Valley Parkway exit at Escondido and drive eleven miles south to inn. Inn is approximately two hours from Los Angeles.

THE INN AT RANCHO SANTA FE
5951 Linea de Cielo (P.O. Box 869)
Rancho Santa Fe, CA 92067
Telephone: (858) 756-1131;
toll-free: (800) 843-4661
Web site: www.theinnatrsf.com

THE INN AT RANCHO SANTA FE

Few Southern Californian inns have matured as gracefully as The Inn at Rancho Santa Fe. In operation for more than seventy years and family operated since the 1950s, The Inn still owes much of its success to the steady guiding hand of the Royce family, which has run the property for three generations.

Boasting some twenty acres of lovingly tended grounds, The Inn is a town landmark and a source of pride for the locals. Palms, magnolias, and citrus trees, as well as expanses of lush lawn, are nurtured by a small army of gardeners. The grounds are in constant bloom.

Also in abundance are towering eucalyptus trees, planted around the turn of the century by the Santa Fe Railroad as a source for railroad ties. The experiment failed when eucalyptus was found unsuitable for that purpose, and the railroad set its sights on real estate. The company began selling residential lots and built an adobe guest house to accommodate prospective buyers. The tile-roofed structure now serves as the Inn's main building.

ROOMS FOR ROMANCE

You won't find frilly canopies, coordinated wallpapers, or multilayered bed coverings here. The Inn continues to decorate its guest rooms in a comfy, traditional style. The kitchenettes and glass-doored cupboards found in many rooms are especially reminiscent of the property's early days, when famous guests like Douglas Fairbanks, Howard Hughes, Mary Pickford, and Errol Flynn relaxed here.

The Inn's preeminent accommodations are the spacious Spanish-style red-tile-roofed Cottages and Cottage Suites (from around $400), which boast kitchens, living rooms, and up to three bedrooms. Offered in the mid $200 range, the smaller Deluxe Cottage Rooms are also fine choices for a romantic getaway. These have fireplaces, kitchenettes or wet bars, sitting areas, and king-sized beds. Cozy Cottage Guest Rooms with fireplaces, king-sized beds, and sitting areas with two chairs are offered in the upper $100 range.

Most of the rooms in the main building ($100 range) have large windows with nice garden views, hardwood floors, and sitting rooms.

THE FACTS

Seventy-seven rooms and casitas, each with private bath. Five swimming pools and four spas. Six lighted tennis courts. Putting green, bocce ball, shuffleboard and croquet courts. Golf course nearby. Horseback riding. Bicycle rentals. Fitness center. Day spa. Two restaurants; one requires more formal dress. Disabled access. Two-night minimum stay required during weekends; three-night minimum stay during holiday periods. Expensive to deluxe.

GETTING THERE

La Casa del Zorro is approximately ninety minutes northeast of San Diego and three hours southeast of Los Angeles. Resort is located about five minutes from Borrego Springs. Directions vary depending on whether you're driving from the Los Angeles or San Diego area. We recommend consulting the resort's Web site for specific driving directions.

LA CASA DEL ZORRO

Like the fabled sirens of the sea who beckoned sailors with their irresistible song, this venerable resort has been luring desert visitors for generations with its acres of perennially luxuriant green. The destination that helped put Borrego Springs on the map, La Casa del Zorro has been welcoming guests since the late 1930s. The property has grown and matured over the years and today covers more than forty desert-defying acres bursting with gardens and boasting five swimming pools and four spas. It's a property truly befitting of the overused term *oasis*.

In addition to swimming, La Casa del Zorro offers multiple recreation options that include horseback riding, bicycling, tennis, and even bocce ball. There's a fitness center and day spa on site, and an adjacent eighteen-hole golf course welcomes resort guests. There are two restaurants, including a more formal dining room that encourages guests to dress up.

ROOMS FOR ROMANCE

In addition to more traditional, two-story guest room buildings, the resort is dotted with more than a dozen freestanding casitas, each ranging in size from one to four bedrooms. Some have private spas and swimming pools; two have baby grand pianos.

For a romantic getaway, we recommend a deluxe poolside room (low to high $300 range). These are furnished with either one king-sized bed or two queen-sized beds and feature dressing rooms, nicely furnished sitting areas, and fireplaces. Downstairs rooms have private patios while those upstairs have balconies overlooking one of the resort's swimming pools.

The resort's one-bedroom casitas (low to high $300 range) are also well suited for romance. These have microwave ovens, small refrigerators, a separate living room, and a dining area.

For a truly memorable romantic experience, consider an elegant one-bedroom casita with a separate living room, a dining area, and your own private outdoor spa. These carry rates starting at about $400. Two-bedroom casitas with private pools are available in the $700 range.

LA CASA DEL ZORRO
3845 Yaqui Pass Road
Borrego Springs, CA 92004
Telephone toll-free: (800) 824-1884
Web site: www.lacasadelzorro.com

Index

MORE RESOURCES FOR ROMANTIC TRAVELS

WEEKENDS FOR TWO IN NORTHERN CALIFORNIA: 50 ROMANTIC GETAWAYS
The original romantic travel guide that started it all, completely revised and updated.

MORE WEEKENDS FOR TWO IN NORTHERN CALIFORNIA: 50 ROMANTIC GETAWAYS
The popular sequel, now in its second edition.

WEEKENDS FOR TWO IN THE WINE COUNTRY: 50 ROMANTIC NORTHERN
CALIFORNIA GETAWAYS
*The newest romantic getaway guide featuring intimate destinations in Napa, Sonoma, and Mendocino
Counties, as well as the Gold Country and the Central Coast.*

WEEKENDS FOR TWO IN THE PACIFIC NORTHWEST: 50 ROMANTIC GETAWAYS
*Coastal, mountain, and island hideaways in Oregon, Washington, and southern British Columbia.
Completely revised and updated with all-new photography in 2003.*

WEEKENDS FOR TWO IN NEW ENGLAND: 50 ROMANTIC GETAWAYS
Places of the heart in Maine, Vermont, New Hampshire, Massachusetts, Connecticut, and Rhode Island.

WEEKENDS FOR TWO IN THE SOUTHWEST: 50 ROMANTIC GETAWAYS
Enchanting destinations in Arizona, New Mexico, and the Four Corners Region.

With more than 150 color photographs and hundreds of room descriptions in each book, these
are the definitive travel guides to the nation's most romantic destinations. All are authored by
Bill Gleeson and published by Chronicle Books. For updates on the *Weekends for Two* series, please visit
www.billgleeson.com.

CAST YOUR VOTE! SOUTHERN CALIFORNIA'S MOST ROMANTIC HOTEL OR INN

Complete and mail this form to Bill Gleeson, *Weekends for Two,* Chronicle Books, 85 Second Street,
Sixth Floor, San Francisco, CA 94105.

Our favorite Southern California romantic retreat (does not have to be featured in this book):

NAME OF HOTEL/INN: _____

CITY/TOWN: _____

THIS PLACE IS SPECIAL BECAUSE: _____

_____

_____